33 HADITHS

33 HADITHS

FOR YOUNG READERS

Compiled & Commented by
İsmail Gökçe

TUGHRA
BOOKS

New Jersey

Originally published in Turkish as *Gençler için 33 Hadis ve Açıklamaları* in 2010

17 16 15 14   2 3 4 5

Published by Tughra Books
345 Clifton Ave., Clifton,
NJ, 07011, USA

www.tughrabooks.com

Library of Congress Cataloging-in-Publication Data Available

ISBN: 978-1-59784-312-6

Printed by
Imak Ofset, Istanbul - Turkey

Contents

Introduction

*Y*outh is the most important and critical stage in one's life. As a matter of fact, everyone should keep this critical period of time in mind. The reason for this is because young people tend to go through major changes in their education, their cultures, and their mentalities. In fact, one's future can be molded and shaped in this age. In this period, a person begins to comprehend his responsibilities towards his family, community, country, and humanity; his personality, identity, and character are all crafted in this time period. Among other things, people tend to pick up their habits during their youth. In the period when young people make important decisions regarding their futures, they will also gain the love for Allah, may His glory be exalted, and the noble Prophet, peace and blessings be upon him, the basic dynamics of ethics, the values of education, the responsibilities towards their religion, and a sense of morality.

Young people today have a variety of problems. We have established a study to help direct young people in overcoming these problems, to demonstrate the things they should be cautious of during their youth, to show them how to become a young person that Allah and His Prophet will be fond of, to explain the dangers of a young person's eagerness and desires, and to emphasize how a single sin in a person's youth, can have dangerous outcomes in the future.

We would like to consider the following verse:

> (In the beginning), none save a young generation among his people truly believed in and followed Moses, for (they were in) fear that the Pharaoh and the chiefs among them (who

collaborated with the Pharaoh in order not to lose their wealth) would subject them to persecutions. The Pharaoh was indeed a haughty tyrant in the land, and he was, indeed, one of those who commit excesses. (Yunus 10:83)

With the combination of a young person's faith, intelligence, body strength, and bravery, even withstanding a tyrant like the Pharaoh becomes possible. We also need young people with these qualities to resist the waves of corruption in our age.

In this project, we gave an effort to display the noble Prophet's *hadiths* that address both, males and females, that is all of young people by providing translations and clarifications. We have included a limited amount of *hadiths*, which address Muslims of all ages, but are more geared towards advising the youth.

During the preparation of this study, we were attentive to make use of the *hadith* corpus, relevant sources, and even annotations of these *hadiths* when needed. Moreover, we have evaluated the *hadiths* within this study, mostly from the perspective that relates to young persons. The *hadiths* have not been extensively explained and the explanations for the *hadiths* have been kept within the boundaries regarding young people, because our intention is to present advice and Prophetic appreciations for them.

It is we who must show effort, but it is Allah the Almighty, Who places the ultimate and ever constant truth in our hearts and grants us success.

- 1 -

The Young Person That Allah Is Pleased with

تَعَجَّبَ رَبُّكَ مِنَ الشَّابِّ لَيْسَتْ لَهُ صَبْوَةٌ

"Allah, is pleased with a young person, who is not prone to temporary pleasures, dedicates his youth to Himself (by obeying His commands), and is not after illicit pleasures." [1]

This *hadith*, by directly addressing the youth, informs that Allah is pleased and content with chivalrous souls, who are not prone to worldly affairs when it comes to living and abiding by one's religion, who do not go through any kind of deviation in fulfilling religious principles, and who stand against the traps of Satan and the carnal soul.

"Will such a young person never slip, never fall, or commit a sin? Of course, even the most auspicious young people may occasionally slip and fall. Occasionally stumbling, sometimes slipping, from place to place, collapsing and being deceived by Satan and falling into a pit of sins is subject to every person except Prophets. However, a gallant young person, who is focused on good deeds, will quickly rush

---

[1]   Ahmad ibn Hanbal, *Musnad*, 4/151; Tabarani, *Al-Mujamu'l-Kabir*, 17/309; Haysami, *Majmau'z-Zawaid*, 10/477; *Musnad al-Haris*, 2/986; Abdullah ibn Mubarak, *Zuhd*, 1/118; *Musnad ash-Shihab*, 1/336; Ajluni, *Kashfu'l-Khafa*, 1/286, 748

to his Prayer rug whenever he is tempted to commit a sin, thereby never allowing his desire for perversion to take control of him and choking it with his repentance and getting rid of the filth of the sin by committing good and righteous deeds, such as Prayers, fasting, and promoting the faith."[2]

Indeed, the most auspicious young person is the one, who constantly remembers death and lives for the Hereafter, and does not become a slave to youthful and carnal desires. Whoever lives his adolescent years in worship and servanthood towards his Lord is very precious.

In light of this, another important quality of the most benevolent young person is that, like Prophet Joseph, peace be upon him, even the most brilliant and joyful situation of this world should not cause him to become heedless, and he is captivated by the ordinary beauties, and he does not surrender to his carnal desires while always living his life for the Hereafter.

Is there anything more important than your Lord's content and sacred love? To gain Allah's content is to follow the path of His beloved Messenger and the eminent Companions, who have endured many sacrifices for religion.

Indeed, today's youth must possess Abu Bakr's fidelity and submission, Umar's justice, Uthman's modesty and munificence, and Ali's faith, knowledge, and love for striving in Allah's cause. They should live like Abdu'r-Rahman ibn Awf, a devout who does not become weary of giving and sacrificing in the path of Allah. They should be like Abu Ubaydah ibn Jarrah, who was a brave man of integrity. They should try to be like Bilal al-Habashi, who was persistent in his faith, like Abdullah ibn Umar, who was a devoted lover of the Prophet and his Sunnah (the actions and words of the Prophet), like Mus'ab ibn Umayr, who was a hero that left the attractive beauties of the transient worldly life by choosing the content of Allah,

---

[2] Gülen, M. Fethullah, *Prizma*, v. 3, pp. 91–94

like Abdullah ibn Abbas, who was an eminent scholar, and like Abu Talha, who was very generous and charitable.

Today, we are in great need of young Companions of the Prophet. Today, we are in dire need of Muadhs, Hudhayfas, Usamas, and Hasan and Husayns. These are the people that the whole humanity needs, and these people will rise from our youth.

-2-

Repentance Is Good, However If It Exists in the Youth, It Is Better

سِتَّةُ أَشْيَاء حَسَنٌ وَلَكِنْ فِي سِتَّةٍ مِنَ النَّاسِ أَحْسَنُ :
اَلْعَدْلُ حَسَنٌ وَلَكِنْ فِي ٱلْأُمَرَاءِ أَحْسَنُ وَالسَّخَاءُ حَسَنٌ وَلَكِنْ فِي
ٱلْأَغْنِيَاءِ أَحْسَنُ وَالْوَرَعُ حَسَنٌ وَلَكِنْ فِي الْعُلَمَاءِ أَحْسَنُ وَالصَّبْرُ
حَسَنٌ وَلَكِنْ فِي الْفُقَرَاءِ أَحْسَنُ وَالتَّوْبَةُ حَسَنٌ وَلَكِنْ فِي الشَّبَابِ
أَحْسَنُ وَالْحَيَاءُ حَسَنٌ وَلَكِنْ فِي النِّسَاءِ أَحْسَنُ

"There are six good things. However, these six things are better if they are represented by particular people: Justice is good, but if executives are just, it is even better. Munificence is good; however, if it is seen among the wealthy, it is even better. Being meticulous in religion (to have abstinence, to stay away from doubtful matters) is good, however, if it is seen among scholars, it is even better. Forbearance is good; however, if it is seen among the poor, it is even greater. Repentance is good; however, if it is seen among the youth, it is even better. Modesty is good; however, if it is seen among women, it is even better." [3]

---

[3] Ali al-Muttaqi, *Kanzu'l Ummal*, 15/1349, 16/175; Munawi, *Fayzu'l-Qadir*, 4/378; Suyuti, *Jamiu's-Saghir*, 8292

This *hadith* explains that some conditions, attitudes, and behaviors are better in certain people. Our intention in including this *hadith* is that, the Messenger of Allah indicates that repentance made by a young person is very noteworthy. In that case, in the eyes of Allah the most auspicious young person is the one that dedicates himself to worship and devotion in order to attain Allah's consent, and one that purges himself of sin by repenting right away.

Like all human beings, young people can also make mistakes and commit sins. Allah's Messenger mentioned that, "Every human commits sin. The best of sinners are those who repent (turn back from their mistakes regretfully)." (*Sunan at-Tirmidhi*). In this *hadith*, our Prophet makes it clear how important a young person's repentance is. The noble Prophet has mentioned that a person is always prone to making mistakes and falling into the pits of sins. For this reason, a young person's repentance is more valuable than other repentance in the eyes of Allah.

Indeed, a young man who has promised to live his life in the path of righteousness, must race to his Prayer rug the moment he commits a sin. He must know how to purge his mistakes. A young person who cleans himself from the filth of his sins by committing activities such as Daily Prayers, fasting, giving alms, and faithful services has performed a great fortitude.

Throughout history, there have been chivalrous souls who have raced to give alms, drawn close to their Prayer rugs and bent double in front of Allah the Almighty, and with their teardrops, have dissolved the filth of their sins. To protect their hearts from the poisonous arrows of Satan and to repent immediately were the most prominent attributes of these heroes of willpower.

Repentance should not be seen as a few simple words. True repentance is, seeking forgiveness through words while feeling the agony of the sins that were committed and being regretful of the mistakes they have made. As a matter of fact, performing supererogatory worship (that brings one closer to Allah), apart from obligatory worship, will cleanse one's heart. Also, it aims to immediately clear the remains of the sins that were committed by that individual.

- 3 -

Young People Who
Are like Angels

مَا مِنْ شَابٍ يَدَعُ لَذَّةَ الدُّنْيَا وَلَهْوَهَا وَيَسْتَقْبِلُ بِشَبَابِهِ طَاعَةَ
الله إِلاَّ أَعْطَاهُ اللهُ أَجْرَ اثْنَيْنِ وَسَبْعِينَ صِدِّيقاً ثُمَّ قَالَ يَقُولُ الله
تَعَالَى أَيُّهَا الشَّابُّ التَّارِكُ شَهْوَتَهُ لِي الْمُبْتَذِلُ شَبَابَهُ لِي أَنْتَ
عِنْدِي كَبَعْضِ مَلائِكَتِي

*"When a young person is brought up with knowledge and worship
and matures in this manner, Allah will give him the reward of seventy-
two loyal people on the Judgment Day. The All-Holy Allah is proud of
such a young person and says: 'O My young servant who does not
obey his evil commanding soul! O My young servant who dedicates
his youth to Me! You are like some of My angels before Me.'"* [4]

after being addressed so compassionately by Allah the Almighty
as expressed in this *hadith*, a young person is expected to find
his purpose in this life.

---

[4] Abu Nuaym, *Hilyatu'l-Awliya*, 4/139, 5/237; Ali al-Muttaqi, *Kanzu'l-Ummal*,
15/1201, 43106, 43107

There is another similar *hadith*: "In the eyes of Allah, the breaths of those who are fasting are much sweeter than the scent of musk. Your Lord, may His glory be exalted, says: To gain My consent, My servants have abandoned their lust, food, and drinks. "Fasting is for Me, and I shall reward for it."[5]

Is there anything greater than becoming the recipient of Allah's address? It is such an honor to be what Allah calls "My young people!" It is such a sublime achievement to attain that position. A wise person is the one who settles accounts in this world and works for the world that comes after death. As for the indolent ones, they waste their time pursuing their carnal desires. In that case, to not become Satan's toy, one must surpass temporary pleasures and aim to obtain the true everlasting contentment of Allah.

In order for you not to fall in the trap of your carnal soul, you must be resilient against the endless desires of the evil commanding soul and restrain your carnal desires. Support the poor; feed the hungry hearts with spiritual richness; be a hope for the hopeless, a remedy for the helpless; in short, lead a decent and virtuous life without falling into the trap of fame and turbulence of rage and greed.

---

[5] Ahmad ibn Hanbal, *Musnad*, 2/395; Abdu'r-Razzak, *Musannaf*, 4/306; Bayhaqi, As-Sunan al-Kubra, 4/304

-4-

Respect for Elders

ما أَكْرَمَ شَابٌّ شَيْخاً لِسِنِّهِ إِلاَّ قَيَّضَ الله لَهُ مَنْ

يُكْرِمُهُ عِنْدَ سِنّه

"If a young person shows respect to someone because of his age, Allah will definitely give him generous people when he grows old." [6]

The noble Messenger also says: "He is not one of us who dies without having shown kindness to our young ones and respect to our older ones."[7]

In this statement, Allah's Messenger has informed us that it is crucial that Muslim youth show respect to their elders. Remember the Golden Rule: One should treat others as one would like others to treat oneself. In this respect, today's youth are tomorrow's elderly; if one wants to live his elderliness in respect, he must show respect to elders in his youth. Even though respect should not be awaited for, it can be earned. One who shows respect will receive respect in return.

This *hadith* informs that one, who shows reverence, will be rewarded with respect in his elderliness. This is how Allah intends to

---

[6]   *Sunan at-Tirmidhi*, Birr, 75
[7]   *Sunan at-Tirmidhi*, Birr, 15; *Sunan Abu Dawud*, Adab, 66

honor those who are respectful to their elders. The matter that is addressed in this *hadith* is the fact that one who is respectful to his elders will be rewarded for his good deeds in this world as well as in the Hereafter.

It is evident that in a society where the elderly show clemency towards the young and the young show respect to the elders, love and reverence among the people shine strongly. This *hadith,* which emphasizes the moral responsibility, also portrays one of the basic pillars which support and hold together the whole society.

In this case, it is necessary that every Muslim should take notice of the elderly, show them respect, and serve them in every way possible. In doing so, the love and respect found in society will be enhanced. Generations will live their lives in a joyful and friendly environment.

Young people should never forget that the elderly today were young once, and that a person's youth is not perpetual, and that there will come a day where they will also become elderly.

The young should acknowledge their adults, and should only show the same respect that they expect to receive in their elder years. Respect is not anticipated, but rather, it is earned. The elderly should be seen as people that possess great experience and should be given their proper value and respect in all societies.

Our children learn from the way we act: They look at the way their parents act toward the elderly and imitate it. If we expect our children to treat us kindly as elders, then we must show them the correct path to do so. Cherishing our elderly is an opportunity to pay our duty and set a good example for our youth. Mothers and fathers who will sacrifice their lives because of the great compassion they hold, should be served and shown respect with sincerity instead of being indifferent towards them. In doing so, one should try to earn their consent and keep them pleased. One who shows respect will earn respect in return. One who shows goodness will earn goodness and be shown it in return.

-5-

The Most Auspicious Young People

خَيْرُ شَبَابِكُمْ مَنْ تَشَبَّهَ بِكُهُولِكُمْ، وَشَرُّ
كُهُولِكُمْ مَنْ تَشَبَّهَ بِشَبَابِكُمْ

"The best of the young among you are those who resemble the old in care and avoidance of vice, while the worst of your elderly are those who imitate the young in vice and heedlessness." [8]

Compared to young people, the elderly are more cautious when it comes to avoiding matters of evil or that can lead to evil. Young people, compared to the elderly, feel freer in complying with their desires. Referring to the characteristics of the young and elderly, this *hadith* expresses that the most auspicious young person is the one who is like an elder and the most malicious elder is the one who is like a young person.

"Whether it is a female or male, the most auspicious young person is the one who constantly thinks about death and the Hereafter so that he can make the necessary preparations for the Hereafter. He

---

8   Tabarani, *Mujamu'l Kabir*, 22/83; Abu Yala, *Musnad*, 13/389; Bayhaqi, *Shu'ab al-Iman*, 6/168

is not a slave of his desires. He is like an elder who is at death's door. Even when evil thoughts and carnal desires are overflowing, such a young person is able to control these feelings with his enthusiasm for the spiritual realms and, and dedicate himself to the path of Allah."

Thus, a virtuous young person does not turn a blind eye to the fact that he is a traveler heading toward the Hereafter, even when he is driven by the desires of the flesh. Such a young person will live like a perishing old man whose hair and beard have turned gray, and dedicate himself to the service of humanity, faith, and the Qur'an. He is similar to a mature man of heart who is not distracted by the innumerable tricks and wiles of Satan, revolting against all corporeal whims, carnal desires, and sins."[9]

A young person who grows unhappy for the religiously forbidden act that he commits out of his momentary heedlessness and feels utter regret, telling himself, "Woe to me, as I am ruined to commit this sin after I have been exposed to many blessings and favors of Allah," and climbs the true stairway of servitude towards Allah, through the steps of repentance, penitence, and withdrawal. Such a young person is a benevolent one who, like an old man, protects his heart against Satan's attacks.

The most auspicious person is the one who chooses the path of Allah. A fortunate person is the one who has targeted the Hereafter, despite the agitating profane pleasures of this world. Indeed, a fortunate person is one uses this world in order to gain the Hereafter.

In summary, the most benevolent young person is the one, who stays focused on death and the Hereafter, like a decent elder does, and who is not smothered by heedlessness of being a slave to the low desires of youth. The worst of the elderly are those who look like the young people in terms of heedlessness and low desires, and submit themselves to carnal desires in a childish manner.

---

[9]   Gülen, M. Fethullah, *Prizma*, v. 3, pp. 91–94

– 6 –

Advice from Our Prophet to a Group of Young People

أَتَيْنَا رَسُولُ اللهِ صَلَّى اللهُ عَلَيْهِ وسَلَّم وَنحْنُ شَبَبَةٌ مُتَقَارِبُونَ، فَأَقمْنَا

عِنْدَهُ عِشْرِينَ لَيْلَةً، وكانَ رَسُولُ اللهِ صَلَّى اللهُ عَلَيْهِ وسَلَّم رَحِيماً

رَفِيقاً، فَظَنَّ أَنَّا قَد اشْتَقْنَا أَهْلَنَا. فَسَأَلَنَا عَمَّنْ تَرَكْنَا مِنْ أَهْلِنَا، فَأَخْبَرْنَاهُ،

فَقال: ارْجِعُوا إلى أَهْلِيكم فَأَقِيمُوا فِيهِمْ، وَعَلِّموهُم وَمُرُوهُمْ، وَصَلُّوا

صَلاةَ كَذا في حِين كَذا، وَصَلُّوا كَذا في حِين كَذا، فإِذَا حَضَرَتِ

الصَّلاةُ فَلْيُؤَذِّنْ لَكُمْ أَحَدُكُمْ، وَلْيَؤُمَّكُم أَكَبْرُكُمْ

*"I came to the Messenger of Allah, peace and blessings be upon
him, with some men from my tribe and stayed with him for twenty
nights. He was kind and merciful to us. When he realized our
longing for our families, he said to us, 'Go back and stay with your
families and teach them the religion, and offer the prayer and one
of you should pronounce the adhan for the Prayer when its time is
due and the oldest one amongst you should lead the Prayer.'"* [10]

---

[10] *Sahih al-Bukhari*, Adhan, 17, 18, 49; Jihad, 42; Adab, 27; *Sahih Muslim*, Masa-jid, 292

This *hadith* contains the great memories and lessons that occurred among a group of young Companions. The narrator of the *hadith*, Malik, learned the way our Prophet used to pray and the steps he used to take to perform Prayer, and then he began teaching people how to pray. Sometimes, he would pray before the time even came in, just to show people how the Prophet used to pray.

Those outstanding young people made an effort to keep away from worldly attractions and absorb the message of the noble Prophet in its entirety. When doing so, in their hearts, they should feel the longing for their family, loved ones, and maybe their children. Since these young people left their homes and countries with these intentions in their hearts, they would surely receive a massive reward from Allah for their migration. Indeed, traveling such distances and using every opportunity they had to learn the teachings of the Qur'an and Sunnah with such sound intentions is truly a blessing. If Allah wills, it is considered a great honor to take part of what the respected Companions of the noble Prophet left behind.

Today, perhaps it is not possible to visit and see our Prophet in person. However, one who makes an effort to deliver the Prophet's messages is in a spiritual atmosphere, and therefore, it is possible to protect themselves from the intrigues of Satan.

A certain concept that we can grasp from this *hadith* is that it is necessary to bear in mind and to please the hearts of family, father, friends, relatives, and children along with other services that one may perform. Through this, we would be attaining the content of our Lord. To withhold spiritual bestowal from your relatives and give it to people that we are not familiar with, goes against the verse, "...*warn your close relatives!*" (ash-Shu'ara 26:214) and the *hadith*, "Help, starting with your kinsmen!"[11] For this reason, while having such an auspicious intention and diligence as going forth in the path of Allah, it is an unexplainable fault to neglect such a matter that Allah and His Messenger have commanded. We are in great need of brave young people that build a harmonious balance between their relationships with their family, relatives, and going forth in the path of Allah.

---

[11] *Sahih Muslim*, Zakah, 38

-7-

The Troubles of Youth

إِنَّ الدُّنْيَا حُلْوَةٌ خَضِرَةٌ وَإِنَّ اللهَ تَعَالَى مُسْتَخْلِفُكُم فِيهَا،
فَيَنْظُرُ كَيْفَ تَعْمَلُونَ فاتَّقُوا الدُّنْيَا واتَّقُوا النِّسَاءَ

"This world is green and sweet. Allah has put you in charge of it so be careful how you behave. Beware of this world and beware of women." [12]

Mentioning that the world is pleasant and appealing explains its attractiveness and charm. When ranking sedition between human beings (the causes of trial), the gains of this life, property, wealth, and rage for promotion and position tend to come first. In the *hadith*, the word "world" is understood as "asset and possession." Just as the taste of fruit and assets are transient, the world is also transient. For this reason, it is considerably wrong for a Muslim to set his heart on this world. The action that needs to be taken is to endeavor for the Hereafter and not to forget the portion of the world. To not set one's heart in this world is more of a significant matter for youth who assume that they have a longer life to live than the elderly who believe that there is a short journey to the Hereafter.

---

[12] *Sahih Muslim*, Dhikr, 99

Indeed, an auspicious young person is the one, who does not gear his mind and thought towards the appealing charms of this world, and who is dedicated to the eternal life in the Hereafter.

Umar ibn al-Khattab once said: "If a person has one bad habit out of nine good habits, it will corrupt all of them. In that case, stay away from the troubles of youth slips."

Today, the youth have many problems and factors that affect the very existence of these problems. Some of these factors are family, friends, school and education, the surrounding atmosphere, and the mass communication. Social circles and mass communication are two of the most influential sources of troubles in young people today.

It is possible to say that, within means of communication fall the radio, television, cinemas, computers, and the internet. Nowadays, these mediums tend to have a great impact and influence on the youth. Not only will informational resources such as books, magazines, and newspapers, provide information, but they will also provide guidance. Let us not forget that nowadays especially, these resources are incentives for demoralization.

These factors breed certain dangers in youth, in which this *hadith* cautions them to stay away from dangers such as the usage of alcohol and drugs, adultery and prostitution, unearned gain and theft, misleading identity, infirmity in faith, and absence of worship and servitude in one's life. Surely, if one avoids such dangers, then they will surely become the people that Allah is pleased with.

In that case, families have to be good role models for their children, raise them in a good manner, work at becoming balanced in terms of material and moral aspects, teach them the importance of responsibility, keep them away from atrocious circles of friends, provide that they read books in their free time, keep them away from alcohol and drug users as well as environments that trigger such dangers, seek ways to create a good relationship with young people, and take the initiative in helping young people socialize. We must strive to keep and protect our cultural and spiritual values.

- 8 -

The Hardest Element in Assessment for Men

مَا تَرَكْتُ بَعْدِي فِتْنَةً هِيَ أَضَرُّ عَلَى الرِّجَالِ مِنَ النِّسَاءِ

"I have not left after me any temptation more harmful to men than women." [13]

*I*n the *hadith*, our beloved Prophet states that towards the End of Times, the biggest sedition (test) for men will be the one they face with the opposite sex.

The greatest dangers and the hardest test that today's youth face, is the ignorance of the sedition and tests they face with the opposite sex. We can see that even the modest young person, who has no trouble protecting oneself from great sins; is defeated against the test he faces with women. Because this sedition does not assault through a logical perspective, but rather through desires and whims. It is one of the fastest causes that lead people to sin.

The word "temptation" that is mentioned in the *hadith* refers to and has the same meaning as "a test, tribulation, and affliction." It is possible to add demoralization to this meaning. Men should abstain from sedition of women; calamity and malignity as is required wom-

---

[13]   *Sahih al-Bukhari*, Nikah, 17; *Sahih Muslim*, Dhikr, 97

en should also abstain from sedition of men, calamity, and malignity. The issue should be approached from both perspectives. In his *hadiths*, our noble Prophet indicates that men will be exposed to the opposite sex as the most harmful sedition. Throughout history, this test has proven to be one of the hardest on many different civilizations.

There is no greater and harmful sedition than that of the sedition of the opposite sex, for youth in particular, especially those who are distant from atmospheres that trigger the spiritual life and have weak willpower. Sedition of women provokes a person's inner feelings. It will leave one alone with their carnal soul. Allah forbids this, and as a direct result of this, it will come to a point where one feels ashamed and will not be able to purge their whole life.

In another *hadith,* following the statement about the need to avoid worldly affairs was made: One should guard himself or herself from the opposite sex. This situation, in comparison to the elderly, is of greater concern to young people. Sedition of women (element of trial) is subject to younger people. The most important intention of our religion is for men and women to be purified of their carnal desires, the pull they have towards each other, and all manners of forbidden relationships. When this goal is finally met, there will be order and regularity in a society, healthy generations who know their parents will be raised, and the happiness and continuity of domesticity and relationships between men and women will be built on a basis of morals. Furthermore, the charm of this world is also in question. As a matter of fact, it is possible to observe such circumstances, even today.

In certain narrations, Allah's Messenger, in a general sense, avoids the sedition that is the consequence of women. In a particular sense, the Prophet gives an example: The first sedition was in consequence of "women" in the tribe of Simeon. Women are one of the elements of temptation (trial), because of their attractiveness, and the power of lust in both women and men. In that case, everyone, notably young people, should give thought to conditions our religion sets forth in relationships between men and women.

- 9 -

The Inheritors of the Messenger of Allah: Young People

عَنْ أَبِي سَعِيدٍ الْخُدْرِيِّ أَنَّهُ كَانَ إِذَا رَأَى الشَّبَابَ قَالَ: مَرْحَبًا

بِوَصِيَّةِ رَسُولِ اللهِ صَلَّى اللهُ عَلَيْهِ وَ سَلَّمَ أَوْصَانَا رَسُولُ اللهِ

صَلَّى اللهُ عَلَيْهِ وَ سَلَّمَ أَنْ نُوَسِّعَ لَكُمْ فِي الْمَجْلِسِ وَ أَنْ نُفهِمَكُمُ

الْحَدِيثَ فَإِنَّكُمْ خُلُوفُنَا وَ أَهْلُ الْحَدِيثِ بَعْدَنَا

When Abu Said al-Khudri came across some young people, he would address them as follows: "O inheritors of the Messenger of Allah, peace and blessings be upon him. The Messenger of Allah has a will in regards to making room for you in our social gathering and meetings, and reciting hadiths to you. Because, you are our successors and the (people of hadith) that will service the hadith after us." [14]

The youth of today are the futures of nations. A nation that invests in their youth will surely approach tomorrow with great confidence. When we look into the life of our noble Prophet, we can see the value that he gave to the youth, provided all kinds of

---
[14] Bayhaqi, *Shu'ab al-Iman*, 2/275

opportunities on behalf of raising them, and moreover, he gave emphasis to his Companions with regards to raising them properly.

Another prominent matter in the *hadith* is that youth should be raised with a sense of religious familiarity. For the youth, religious knowledge actually provides encouragement for all fields of knowledge; in the expression of the *hadith* and emphasis on "people of *hadith*." This is because the most significant quality in ideal young people we are going to trust our future with is having religious knowledge. Our era is the age of knowledge. Ignorant societies will be unable to escape being putty in someone's hands.

Another important point here is as follows: Our noble Prophet says, "My Companions are like stars; whoever of them you follow, you will be rightly guided."

Consequently, young people who act upon a conscience of knowing this fact, will show superlative exertion and diligence in regards to being worthy of it.

It is for this reason that the noble Ibn Mas'ud embraced young people who requested and set forth in acquiring knowledge by saying, "O candles that illuminate the foundation of knowledge and wisdom and brighten darkness."[15]

The narrator, Abu Said al-Khudri has said to the young people: "O the son of my brother! When in doubt, you can definitely ask me for answers. It is more pleasing for you to attain certainty than for you to be suspicious and curious."

---

[15] Bayhaqi, *Shu'ab al-Iman*, 5, 476

- 10 -

Young People and Eyes
Trespassing on the Forbidden

وَعَنْ جَرِيرٍ رَضِيَ اللهُ عَنْهُ قَالَ: سَأَلْتُ رَسُولَ اللهِ صَلَّى اللهُ

عَلَيْهِ وسَلَّمَ عَنْ نَظَرِ الفجْأَةِ فَقَالَ: «اصْرِفْ بَصَرَكَ»

Jarir ibn Abdullah, may Allah be pleased with him, said: "I asked
the Messenger of Allah, peace and blessings be upon him, about
the unintentional glance. He said, 'Avert your eyes!'" [16]

This *hadith* advises to immediately look away from sudden looks at what is forbidden. Our noble Prophet was asked whether one would be responsible or not for unconscious and sudden looks at a woman where they witness forbidden parts, to which he replied, "Immediately turn your eyes to (another direction)!"

Hence, one is not responsible for this momentary look, but he becomes responsible if he continues looking. Only then will that person have committed a forbidden act. Thus, Allah the Almighty commands that male believers should abstain from looking at what is forbidden.

Let us also take into account the following incident: After the commandment regarding women wearing veils came down, Abdullah ibn

---

[16] *Sahih Muslim*, Adab, 45; *Sunan Abu Dawud*, Nikah, 43; *Sunan at-Tirmidhi*, Adab, 28

Umm Maktum, who was blind, came to our Prophet while he was with his wives Umm Salama and Maymuna. Our noble Prophet commanded them to wear their veils because Ibn Umm Maktum was coming. They said that the man was blind, however our Prophet responded as follows: "Are you two also blind? Don't you see him?" Thus, he stated that not only men, but also women should not look at the forbidden. The Qur'anic verse prescribes, "*Tell the believing women that they (also) should restrain their gaze (from looking at the men whom it is lawful for them to marry, and from others' private parts)*" (an-Nur 24:31). For this reason, it is the responsibility of both, Muslim men and women, to abstain from looking at what is forbidden.

However, it is the responsibility of our Prophet's wives to also veil in the presence of a blind man. This was a special duty of the Prophet's wives. The advice that our Prophet has given to his wives about covering, can be understood as a warning for them not to look at men, even if they are blind. Actually, in the event that they do not feel lust, it is permissible for Muslim women to look at men, except the area between their navel and knee caps. Only if they feel lust should they not look at them. It is recommended to be cautious in regards to the probable mischief that will come about since it is difficult to determine and detect it.

Relevant to this topic, another *hadith* mentions: "The (evil) gaze is a poisonous arrow from the arrows of Iblis. He that abstains from it out of M9y fear, I will grant him in return such faith, the sweetness of which he will experience within his heart."[17]

The part where the *hadith* continues on to say, "Whoever refuses to look at that which is forbidden on account of their fear of Me," is an aforementioned *hadith*. That is to say that our Prophet transferred this from our Almighty Allah. By conveying this complimentary message from Allah, our Prophet is emphasizing and showing us just how important it is to shut our eyes against what is forbidden.

---

[17] Hakim, *Mustadrak*, 4/349; Ahmad ibn Hanbal, *Musnad*, 5/264; Tabarani, *Al-Mujamu'l-Kabir*, 10/173; *Musnad ash-Shihab*,1/195

If it is not treated with repentance, there is no other way to cure the damages that the poisonous arrow causes. The sins that will come about from looking at the forbidden images will lodge into one's heart like an arrow. It is bad enough that the eyes catch sight of what is forbidden. The brave souls are those who do not continue to look and will suppress the arrow that poisons their hearts with repentance.

There is no limit to the amount of reward that Allah the Almighty will give to the one who abstains from looking at what is forbidden. Later on in the *hadith,* it mentions of such elation due to faith that it is possible to experience the true meaning of believing, and from this understanding, one may attain other spiritual beauties.

Another point that is mentioned in the *hadith* is that one should abstain from looking at what is forbidden because of their love for Allah. What better reason is there for anyone to abstain from looking at what is forbidden? Even though this is a different matter, abstaining from something forbidden for the sole purpose of gaining Allah's pleasure is a sign of purity of intention.

Looking at something that is forbidden is the adultery of eyes. Our noble Prophet said, "The fornication of the eyes is looking at that which is forbidden. The fornication of ears is listening to forbidden words. The fornication of the tongue is speaking of what is forbidden. The fornication of the hands is touching the opposite sex in a lustful matter. The fornication of the feet is to go to places that are forbidden. The heart yearns and desires for fornication, and the genitals either confirm it or contradict it."

Our beloved Prophet said, "Every eye shall cry on the Day of Resurrection with the exception of three: an eye which passed the nights guarding Muslims (their wealth, land, etc.) for the sake of Allah; an an eye which wept for fear of Allah; and an eye which was cast down against the deeds made forbidden by Allah."

In another *hadith* that expresses not looking at what is forbidden, the Messenger of Allah, firstly to Ali ibn Abi Talib then to his Ummah (community) said, "O Ali, the first glance is in your favor but the second one is against you."[18]

"As our noble Prophet indicated, because there is no intention, one is not responsible for the first glance, but because the second glance is intended and in a volitional matter, it is emphasized that it will be written as a sin. Even though it is not a sin to glance once, because there is an intention to do so in the second and the following glances, the carnal soul has a role and because it is the first link in the chain, it can pull one into sin. Thus, the path that leads to haram is hindered beforehand.[19]

Our beloved Prophet calls out in specific to the youth, due to their tendency to react to their desires. Today especially, even if it is unintentional, there are unpleasant scenes on the streets that the eye can catch a glimpse of. It is very significant to earn a spiritual reward from worship and it is possible to earn this reward by looking away from what is forbidden and abstaining from doing so the second time.

"Once, the honorable Imam Shafi told his teacher, Waqi ibn Jarrah, that he was experiencing a weakness in memory. His most respected teacher summoned Imam Shafi to stand clear of even the smallest sins and told him: 'Knowledge is a Divine light; Allah the Almighty will not grant His Divine light to one who constantly dives into sin.' Moreover, Imam Shafi probably complained about his weakness of memory after not being able to memorize the material that he was so eager to learn. Also, a soul like Imam Shafi would not sin intentionally."[20]

All Muslims, especially young people, should try their best to stay away from forbidden things and take caution in what they eat and drink. They should stay away from environments that push them towards lust and stress.

---

[18] *Sunan at-Tirmidhi*, 5/1010; *Sunan Abu Dawud*, 1/652

[19] Gülen, M. Fethullah, *İnancın Gölgesinde-2*, (The Essentials of the Islamic Faith-2), "Âfaki Meseleler"

[20] Gülen, M. Fethullah, *Kırık Testi-7, Ölumsuzluk İksiri*, "Mefluç Dimağlar ve Unutkanlığın Reçetesi"

-11-

Young People and
Sexual Deviations

لاَ يَنْظُرُ الرَّجُلُ إِلَى عَوْرَةِ الرَّجُلِ، وَلاَ الْمَرْأَةُ إِلَى عَوْرَةِ الْمَرْأَةِ،

ولاَ يُفْضِي الرَّجُلُ إِلَى الرَّجُلِ فِي ثَوْبٍ وَاحِدٍ، وَلاَ تُفْضِي

الْمَرْأَةُ إِلَى الْمَرْأَةِ فِي الثَّوْبِ الْوَاحِدِ

*"A man should not look at another man's private parts nor a woman at
another woman's private parts. Two men should not lie naked under
the same cover nor two women under the same cover."* [21]

This *hadith* advises to protect and abstain the eyes from the forbidden. In fact, it directly prohibits that individuals of the same gender look at each other's private parts or lay under the same cover. There is no difference between the youth and the elders when it comes to looking at private parts and laying under the same blanket. Also, it is prohibited to be laying nakedly and in contact with one another. On the other hand, it is also prohibited to look at a young and good-looking man with lust. In fact this is even expressed as one of the major sins.

---

[21] *Sahih Muslim*, Hayz, 74; *Sunan at-Tirmizi*, Adab, 38; *Sunan ibn Majah*, Taharat, 137

Even in mandatory situations, such as being treated and bearing witness in court, we are only permitted to look as much as we need to; nothing more and nothing less. To continue looking in a trivial matter is also prohibited. We must also indicate that it is a sin for men and women who do not have a marital bond to look at each other's private parts. According to the Hanafi School, a man's private parts are between their navel and knee caps. As for women, apart from their hands, face, and feet; their whole body is considered to be private.

Acting according to this noble *hadith* that prevents a number of different sins beforehand, will help protect the family life, by sustaining chastity and honor.

The Young Person Who Is Raised in Worship to Allah

سَبْعَةٌ يُظِلُّهُمُ اللهُ فِي ظِلِّهِ يَوْمَ لا ظِلَّ إِلاَّ ظِلُّهُ: إِمَامٌ عَادِلٌ،
وَشَابٌّ نَشَأَ فِي عِبَادَةِ اللهِ عَزَّ وَجَلَّ، وَرَجُلٌ قَلْبُهُ مَعَلَّقٌ
بِالْمَسَاجِدِ وَرَجُلانِ تَحَابَّا فِي اللهِ اجْتَمَعَا عَلَيْهِ، وَتَفَرَّقَا عَلَيْهِ،
وَرَجُلٌ دَعَتْهُ امْرَأَةٌ ذَاتُ مَنْصِبٍ وَجَمَالٍ، فَقَالَ: إِنِّي أَخَافُ
اللهَ، وَرَجُلٌ تَصَدَّقَ بِصَدَقَةٍ، فَأَخْفَاهَا حَتَّى لا تَعْلَمَ شِمَالُهُ مَا
تُنْفِقُ يَمِينُهُ، وَرَجُلٌ ذَكَرَ اللهَ خَالِياً فَفَاضَتْ عَيْنَاهُ

"There are seven whom Allah will shade with His shade on the day when there is no shade but His shade: a just imam (leader), a youth who grows up worshipping Allah, the Mighty and Exalted, a man whose heart is attached to the mosque, two men who love each other for the sake of Allah, meeting and parting for that reason alone, a man who refuses the advances of a noble and beautiful woman, saying, 'I fear Allah', a man who gives sadaqa (alms) and conceals it so that his left hand does not know what his right hand gives, and a man who remembers Allah when he is alone and his eyes overflow with tears." [22]

---

[22] *Sahih al-Bukhari*, Adhan, 36; Zakah, 16; Riqaq, 24; Hudud, 19; *Sahih Muslim*, Zakah, 91

This *hadith* mentions that Allah's Mercy will protect seven different types of people on a day that will be scorching hot. These seven classes are not the only classes of people that will be under Allah's shade. In other *hadiths*, people with different attributes have also been mentioned.[23]

When we look at the attributes of the people mentioned in the *hadith*, we notice that they have overcome and achieved difficult goals, and have given a great effort, despite their internal and external obstacles. Their common attribute is the heroism in servitude that is based on love.

Here we would like to emphasize the young person that is expressed: The young person, who devotes himself to serving Allah at a time of disruption and disorder, despite his corporeal passions and desires… The young person, who was brought up in a climate of worshipping Allah… The young person, who devoted himself to the service of faith and the Qur'an, who did not hinder his worship, who managed to control his carnal desires… Leading such a life is very important. However, carrying this out while in your youth years is even more important.

Being meticulous in worshipping in youth is significant, because it is not easy to perform acts of worship during their youth, a period when people are full of carnal desires.[24]

---

[23] *Sahih Muslim*, Zuhd, 74; Birr, 38; *Sunan at-Tirmidhi*, Buyu, 67; *Sunan ibn Majah*, Sadaqat, 14

[24] Ayni, *Umdatu'l-Qari*, 5/178

- 13 -

Young People and Marriage

يَا مَعْشَرَ الشَّبَابِ مَنِ اسْتَطَاعَ مِنْكُمُ الْبَاءَةَ فَلْيَتَزَوَّجْ فَإِنَّهُ أَغَضُّ

لِلْبَصَرِ وَأَحْصَنُ لِلْفَرْجِ وَمَنْ لَمْ يَسْتَطِعْ فَعَلَيْهِ بِالصَّوْمِ فَإِنَّهُ لَهُ وِجَاءٌ

*"O young people! Whoever among you can marry, should
marry, because it helps him lower his gaze and guard his
modesty and whoever is not able to marry, should fast, as
fasting diminishes his sexual power."* [25]

$\mathcal{A}$llah considers marriage to be proof of His existence, and says: *"And among His signs is that He has created for you, from your selves, mates, that you may incline towards them and find rest in them, and He has engendered love and tenderness between you. Surely in this are signs for people who reflect"* (ar-Rum 30:21). Yes, there are different kinds of marriages, permissible, obligatory reprehensible, and traditional marriages. Scholars of the Islamic Law recommend marriage as soon as possible for those people with a higher potential of action upon their carnal desires, lustful wishes, and breaching the Islamic Law. One of the rea-

---

[25] *Sahih al-Bukhari*, Nikah, 10; *Sahih Muslim*, Nikah, 1; *Sunan Abu Dawud*, Nikah, 1;
Sunan at-Tirmidhi, Nikah, 1; *Sunan an-Nasa'i*, Siyam, 43

sons for the scholars' recommendation regarding marriage is this very *hadith*.

This *hadith* warns against the evil and the unlawful lust because a married person who found a partner that he likes can protect himself from unlawful acts and guard his modesty. Marriage is the safest means of protecting oneself. The verse above talks about the married couples dwelling in tranquility, that is to say that, in a way, married couples should save their attention for one another and not look at others. For this reason, ways leading up to marriage should be simplified and people should help others get married for the sake of Allah.

The *hadith* suggests that people who are unable to get married should fast. Fasting has such an incredible restraining force and it strengthens willpower. It is a form of worship that reduces the lustful wishes while deepening the understanding of the world beyond its material dimensions. Fasting reminds us that true freedom and pleasure lie in being a servant to Allah and submitting only to Him. For that reason, Allah says, "Fasting is for Me, and I shall reward for it." (Divine *hadith*).

At this point, it is important to remember what Tawus ibn Kaysan says about marriage: "The religion of young people is not complete until marriage."[26]

---

[26] Abu Nuaym, *Hilyatu'l-Awliya*, 4/6; Said ibn Mansur, *Sunan*, 1/140

-14-

Privacy and Religious Education

مُرُوا أَوْلادَكُمْ بِالصَّلاةِ وهُمْ أَبْنَاءُ سَبْعِ سِنِينَ، وَاضْرِبُوهُمْ
عَلَيْهَا وَهُمْ أَبْنَاءُ عَشْرٍ، وَفَرِّقُوا بَيْنَهُمْ فِي الْمَضَاجِعِ

*"Tell your children to pray when they are seven, and punish
them (lightly) if they do not do so when they are ten, and
separate their beds."*[27]

his *hadith* offers some recommendations for teaching children how to pray. The first recommendation is teaching the children how to pray at the age of seven. The second recommendation is to seriously warn them at the age of ten. If the children are brought up in families where other members pray, they will start imitating this behavior and begin to pray. It is important to teach children how to pray and increase their consciousness and help them maintain their consistency with Prayers. The reason that some people stop praying when they reach puberty is because of the heedlessness and carnal desires that come to be as part of being a teenager. This can in turn be attributed to lack of conscious education. According to our noble Prophet, children should be taught how to pray at a very young age. Children who receive religious ed-

---

[27] *Sunan Abu Dawud*, Salah, 26

ucation at young ages do not neglect their Prayers when they become teenagers.

Young individuals who did not somehow receive a good religious upbringing or education should be patient with worship, contemplate the advantages of Prayer, and start to take advantage of the Prayer that is considered to be the index of all other forms of prayers. Otherwise, they deserve to be chastised, as clearly mentioned in the *hadith*. The term "punishment" mentioned in the *hadith* should be understood as a light punishment. It does not mean that children should be punished severely and beat mercilessly.

The *hadith* also mentions separating beds. This punishment is about children who are ten. Girls and boys should sleep on different beds and should not share. This is an important practice that prevents confusion about sex and sexuality in children of all ages. It is possible that children who are physically close to others may turn out to have a sense of confusion when it comes to sex and sexuality.

-15-

Youth and Physical Appearance

نَهَى رَسُولُ اللهِ صَلَّى اللهُ عَلَيْهِ وسَلَّم عَنِ القَزَع

*"The Messenger of Allah, peace and blessings be upon him,
forbade shaving part of the head."* [28]

ccording to Abdullah ibn Umar, one day, the Prophet saw a child who had his head shaven in some areas and unshaven in other areas. He forbade the family members from doing this and said: "You either shave it all or you leave it all!"[29]

According to Ali ibn Abi Talib, the beloved Prophet forbade women from completely shaving off their hair.[30]

These *hadith*s tell us the appropriate ways of shaving hair. Our noble Prophet prefers plainness and differentiation from other cultures. Shaving a large part of the head and leaving some parts unshaven is not the way our Prophet taught us to shave. We understand from other *hadith*s that the Prophet disapproves of this shaving method, as it resembles the shavings of some non-Muslims during that time. For this reason, it is obvious that it is not appropriate to import or adapt the physical appearances or cloth-

[28] *Sahih al-Bukhari*, Libas, 72; *Sahih Muslim*, Libas, 72, 113; *Sunan Abu Dawud*, Tarajjul, 14; *Sunan an-Nasa'i*, Zinah, 5, 58; *Sunan ibn Majah*, Libas, 38
[29] *Sunan Abu Dawud*, Tarajjul, 14
[30] *Sunan an-Nasa'i*, Zinah, 4; *Sunan at-Tirmidhi*, Hajj, 75

ing styles from other cultures under the name of fashion. Based on the *hadith,* we can understand that we should adopt the styles that are considered appropriate in our own culture.

Also, another noteworthy aspect is that the noble Prophet used to begin shaving his head from the right side, and work his way to the left.

Our beloved Prophet forbade women from shaving their hair off completely. The only exception to this rule is for health concerns. Otherwise, if a woman shaves off her hair completely, it is as if she cut off a bodily organ.

The young people who try to imitate other people, celebrities, or the fashion icons that appear on magazine covers and TV shows should be more sensitive and accepting of our Prophet's suggestions on this matter.

-16-

Being Young and Possessing Innate Beauty

لَعَنَ اللهُ الْوَاشِمَاتِ وَالْمُسْتَوْشِمَاتِ وَالْمُتَنَمِّصَاتِ،
وَالْمُتَفَلِّجَاتِ لِلْحُسْنِ، الْمُغَيِّرَاتِ خَلْقِ اللهِ، فَقَالَتْ لَهُ امْرَأَةٌ
فِي ذَلِكَ. فَقَالَ: وَمَا لِي لاَ أَلْعَنُ مَنْ لَعَنَ رَسُولُ اللهِ صَلَّى
اللهُ عَلَيْهِ وسَلَّم وَهُوَ فِي كِتَابِ اللهِ؟، قَالَ اللهُ تَعَالَى: {وَمَا
آتَاكُمُ الرَّسُولُ فَخُذُوهُ وَمَا نَهَاكُمْ عَنْهُ فَانْتَهُوا}

Ibn Mas'ud reported, "Allah curses women who tattoo and are tattooed, women who pluck their eyebrows, and women who file their teeth to make gaps for beauty, altering Allah's creation!" A woman spoke to him about that and he said, "Why should I not curse those the Messenger of Allah, peace and blessings be upon him, cursed when that is in the Book of Allah? Allah the Almighty says, 'Whatever the Messenger gives you, accept it willingly; and whatever he forbids you, refrain from it'" (al-Hashr 59:7). [31]

---

[31] *Sahih al-Bukhari*, Tafsiru'l surah (59), 4; Libas, 82, 84, 85, 87; *Sahih Muslim*, Libas, 120, *Sunan Abu Dawud*, Tarajjul, 5; *Sunan at-Tirmidhi*, Adab, 33; *Sunan an-Nasa'i*, Zinat, 24, 26, 71; *Sunan ibn Majah*, Nikah, 52

This is how the event explained in the *hadith* took place: Ibn Mas'ud recited the *hadith* about some women who practiced the mentioned methods to make themselves look beautiful when they had no health concerns or imperative needs for those modifications. A well-known woman by the name of Umm Ya'qub said to Ibn Mas'ud: "I read the Qur'an from the beginning to the end and have never come across anything that cursed women who did such things. Where are you taking all of this from? Ibn Mas'ud said that the Prophet cursed such women and that he will curse the people that the Prophet has cursed. He further explained: "If you, as you said, have really read the Qur'an, you must have come across a verse that explains this matter," and read the verse above *"Whatever the Messenger gives you, accept it willingly; and whatever he forbids you, refrain from it."* Umm Ya'qub did not have anything to come back with or reply to Ibn Mas'ud, but claimed that his wife performs some of those acts. Ibn Mas'ud then told her, "Go and see" and upon seeing, Umm Ya'qub said "I did not see any of these modifications on your wife." Thereupon, Ibn Mas'ud said, "If she did have any of those things, we would not still be together." Even though this *hadith* was said under special circumstances, the message that is found in it applies to all of the believers.

This *hadith* tells us the impropriety of changing the innate beauty. This *hadith* expresses that Allah curses those who deny the beauty that Allah has given them. It is not forbidden to change the physical abnormalities or irregularities that happen as a result of an accident or a disease. What is forbidden is being dissatisfied with what Allah has bestowed upon you and trying to change it.

Nowadays, the inborn desire of women to look beautiful is being exploited, and women are faced with physical and financial difficulties.

If women have facial hair that starts growing on their lips or chins, it is advised that they remove them. However, removing one's eyelashes or eyebrows is forbidden. Rasping in between the front teeth in order to make them seem separated and smaller is also forbidden. However, any action or operation that is carried out to remove an anomaly or a disease is not forbidden.

Another thing we learn from this *hadith* is that following the Sunnah as best as one can is the order of the Qur'an, and more importantly, the order of Allah the Almighty. The Qur'an tells us that the efforts of those who claim, "The Qur'an is enough for us" in order to deviate from the Sunnah are futile. The people who follow the Sunnah of the noble Prophet live according to the Qur'an because the life of the Prophet revolved around the application of the Qur'an in reality.

Also, the Prophet prohibits the pulling out of white hair, as it is the light of Muslims on the Day of Resurrection.[32]

Not pulling out the white hair in one's head is a sign of contentedness with the flow of life, which is determined by Divine Laws. Pulling the white hair in one's head and beard symbolizes the wish to stay young. Trying to appear young when you are not is a kind of hypocrisy. Dying one's hair or beard is not recommended.

We ask Allah for His help and guidance in all matters.

---

[32] *Sunan Abu Dawud*, Tarajjul, 17; *Sunan at-Tirmidhi*, Adab, 56; *Sunan an-Nasa'i*, Zinat, 13

Youth and Exalting the Word of Allah

إِنَّ رَسُولَ اللهِ صَلَّى اللهُ عَلَيْهِ وَسَلَّمَ بَعْدَ مَا هَاجَرَ وَجَاءَ الَّذِينَ

كَانُوا بِأَرْضِ الْحَبَشَةِ بَعَثَ بِعْثَيْنِ قِبَلَ الشَّامِ إِلَى كَلْبٍ وَبُلْقِينَ

وَغَسَّانٍ وَكُفَّارِ الْعَرَبِ الَّذِينَ فِي مَشَارِفِ الشَّامِ فَأَمَرَ رَسُولُ اللهِ

صَلَّى اللهُ عَلَيْهِ وَسَلَّمَ عَلَى أَحَدِ الْبِعْثَيْنِ اَبَا عُبَيْدَةَ بْنَ الْجَرَّاحِ

*After migrating to Mecca and the arrival of the Companions that
were sent to Abyssinia as immigrants, the Messenger of Allah,
peace and blessings be upon him, sent two armed troops to the
tribes of the Kalb, Bulqin and Ghassan as well as to the Arab
disbelievers in the region of Sham. He assigned Abu Ubaydah
ibn Jarrah as the commander for one of these troops.*[33]

The Messenger of Allah had shown a unique example of leadership in engaging people around him with different types of activities. He used to give people the exact positions that suited their skill sets. He used to determine which person pres-

---

[33] Abdu'r-Razzak, *Musannaf*, 5:452; Said ibn Mansur, *Sunan*, 2:317; Bazzar, *Musnad*, 3/204; Ali al-Muttaqi, *Kanz al-Ummal*, 3:1135

ent at the time was perfect to carry out a certain duty. Our noble Prophet discovered the capabilities and talents of his Companions and assigned duties to them accordingly. Because of this, he knew how to utilize energies of individuals in the best ways possible. No individual that lived during the Prophet's time could deny his ability to do this.

Our Prophet did an excellent job educating individuals from his Companions to follow his path. These Companions in turn helped educate the rest of the Prophet's community to remain on the same path. On the path of conquering the hearts, the Messenger of Allah educated some of the greatest people, including Khalid, Uqba, Ahnaf, Tariq, and Muhammad ibn Qasim.

By appointing such great and young individuals, like Abu Ubayda ibn Jarrah and Usama ibn Zayd to lead armies and troops,[34] the Messenger merely displayed the importance and the duties of youth in spreading the Word of Allah all over the world. In doing so, he drastically increased the youth's confidence. It was a Golden Age when the Companions of the Messenger like Abu Bakr, Umar, Uthman, Ali, Khalid, Sa'd, Abu Ubayda, and Ala al-Khadrami, may Allah be pleased with them, and hundreds more were fully utilized, without any talent or skill set being wasted.

We would surely gasp in awe if we were to begin to consider the capabilities of the youth and the responsibilities given to them at the time of the noble Prophet. They were so great that many adults today would not carry out and hold the same responsibilities as many young Companions did at the time.

---

[34] *Sahih al-Bukhari*, Fadailu'l-Ashab, 17, Maghazi, 42, 87, Ayman 2, Ahkam, 33; *Sahih Muslim*, Fadailu's-Sahaba, 63

-18-

Considering Youth as a Blessing

اِغْتَنِمْ خَمْساً قَبْلَ خَمْسٍ: شَبَابَكَ قَبْلَ هَرَمِكَ، وَصِحَّتَكَ
قَبْلَ سَقَمِكَ، وَغِنَاءَكَ قَبْلَ فَقْرِكَ، وَفَرَاغَكَ قَبْلَ شُغْلِكَ،
وَحَيَاتَكَ قَبْلَ مَوْتِكَ

"Take advantage of five matters before five other matters: your youth, before you become old; and your health, before you fall sick; and your richness, before you become poor; and your free time before you become busy; and your life, before your death."[35]

ach and every aspect of the *hadith* mentioned above can surely apply to everyone's life. They are like phases that individuals go through. One needs to know the vast value of youth before he or she reaches old age. Old people are those who know best the value of youth. Whether we like it or not, one day, everyone will get old. It happens every second, every minute, and every hour of every single day. The most important thing here is to know the value of youth before entering the stage of senility. Many young people today have a very negative attitude towards their youth phase. They approach it by saying, "Let me enjoy my youth and I'll figure out everything else

---

[35] Hakim, *Mustadrak*, 4:341; Ibn Abi Shayba, *Musannaf*, 7:77; Bayhaqi, *Shuabu'l-Iman*, 7:263; *Hilyatu'l-Awliya*, 4:148

when I get older." Many people have said that before and many people continue to approach their youth in this manner. Surely, this is not the proper attitude. However, worshipping and spreading the Word of Allah all over the world by great individuals, usually go hand-in-hand with being young in age and soul.

You have probably seen many older individuals who regret how they spent their years. A very well-known proverb that is mentioned in many books and translated into a number of different languages, reads, "I wish my youth would return to me so that I could tell it the troubles that serenity has caused me." We need to use the power of our young ages and the dynamism of our adolescence in such a way to convey the beauties of our religion, taught by Allah, to other people. This way, we will not be among those people who mourn at the end of the day, wishing for our youth to return. Truly, the value of worship and servitude to Allah performed in a healthy and vigorous state is very special and spiritually rewarding. If to think about religious practices performed without any efforts in youth, then we can understand here what favors our youth hold. Indeed, performing worship in the way our hearts desire is possible in our young ages. When we reach old age, when our backs begin bending into humps and our bodies weaken, we will start facing difficulties in social life as well as in accomplishing religious practices.

Those who know the real value of life plan to accomplish a number of auspicious things throughout it. At the time when strength can fall into step with religious longing and desire, many things can be done in the path of Allah. During the period of maturity and senility, there are plenty of deeds like engaging with family and children, and taking care of health problems; these all may hinder our bustling about in servitude of Allah. Therefore, we need to consider our youth as a capital given by Allah, and find ways of spending this period of our lives profitably and productively.

Poverty is considered a shortage, which is why one needs to be patient. On the flip side, at the time when a person gains wealth, then he should keep in mind the previous state that he was in, and act accordingly to show his thankfulness and gratitude.

Knowing the value of health before illness is also, to one extent, being grateful for a healthy state. Knowing the value of leisure time is generally known by whenever they get too busy. The most general meaning of all those matters is a necessity of knowing the value of life before passing away. It is necessary to get a move on doing good deeds in our youth without losing even a single moment of time. Our noble Prophet decreed the following in one of his *hadiths*:

"Hasten to do good deeds before you are overtaken by one of the seven afflictions." Then (giving a warning) he said, "Are you waiting for such poverty which will make you unmindful of devotion; or prosperity which will make you corrupt, or disease as will disable you, or such senility as will make you mentally unstable, or sudden death, or Ad-Dajjal who is the worst expected absent, or the Last Day, and the Last Day will be most grievous and most bitter?"[36]

In this *hadith* that brought clarity to a topic that we tried to explain, it is advised to take measures before facing possible events. If to consider those seven things, then it becomes obvious that a period, where we should take measures, is mainly youth. Many old people surely have faced a few of those things already. However, if a person is alive and still has time to live according to causes, then that person needs to take measures (till his last breathe). In fact, things that a person had not even thought of or expects to have may come suddenly and unexpectedly. Hence, youth is a period of life that should be appraised and used in the best way possible.

It is necessary to be conscious, alert, and act wisely at an age that we have an opportunity, strength and power. The aspects described in the *hadith* above are very remarkable: Poverty makes us forget limits of forbidden and allowed set by, wealth pulls us astray, illness destroys the normal flow of life and flips all of our feelings upside down, senility makes us talk about nonsense, death comes all of a sudden, and the coming of Ad-Dajjal, who is the most evil and dangerous sign of the End Times, and finally, the Last Day, troubles and pain of which will be unbearable...

---

[36] *Sunan at-Tirmidhi*, Zuhd, 3

Sometimes, a person cannot do anything he wants to. We should accomplish some things and bustle about on right path before it is too late. The responsibilities of our families lie on our shoulders. All these things are possible only in our youth. For that reason, there are people, who postpone their marriage. Furthermore, if to think about *hadith*, then it is impossible for a person to commit an evil deed.

The Messenger of Allah informed us that those, who postpone their work continuously, or in other words, procrastinators, will be perished. In addition to this, the Messenger of Allah stated that there are two favors of Allah on humans, the value to which people are ignorant. One of those two favors is leisure time. A Muslim should always be lively and have energy to do some beneficial activities. There are many among us, who said in their youth, "I will do it later on, I'm still too young now," and wasted it completely. In doing so, we are merely deceiving ourselves. There are plenty of good deeds to be done, but by postponing them, how will we be able to handle them all at the end of our lives?

Truly, we need to get used to bustling about in the right path so that we don't just hang around and then regret that for the rest of our lives. It will be a significant means of personal as well as social development and progress. Sometimes, a person criticizes acts done in his or her youth. Here is another *hadith* of our noble Prophet that better explains:

"The son of Adam will not pass away from Allah until he is asked about five things: how he lived his life, and how he utilized his youth, with what means did he earn his wealth, how did he spend his wealth, and what did he do with his knowledge."[37]

Indeed, the Hereafter is earned in this world. Whatever you sow in this life, you will surely reap it in the Hereafter. On the Day of Resurrection, everyone will be questioned about his deeds done in this world. Five deeds mentioned in the *hadith* above are the most important matters that concern the Hereafter. For sure there are other things that a person would be questioned about. However,

---

[37] *Sunan at-Tirmidhi*, Qiyamah, 1

alongside with their being matters of concern for everyone, among worldly deeds and rush, they comprise many events that are not made a reckoning of.

Each person will be questioned about where he spent his life. We could possibly relate and begin to explain this based on each phase of life, whereas a useful reckoning that will result in preparing to the Hereafter, should be possible if it had been started to be made in youth. As for the question of spending one's life, then the most conspicuous point here is how the youth was spent. In order to prepare for that question, we need to spend the prime of our lives according to Allah's content. Another matter that will be questioned is the matter of gained knowledge and usage of that knowledge (how much and where). How we earned our money and where we spend it is another question. Indeed our youth is a crucial period of life that will provide positive answers to all the questions.

Yes, on the Day of Resurrection, people will be brought to account and held responsible for each and every deed they committed in this world. We need to approach this worldly life as a favor from Allah the Almighty for making preparations with our deeds for the Hereafter. Therefore, we need to spend the most productive period of our lives, our youth, pleasing Allah and keeping in mind the truth of our being interrogated, we must comprehend that very fact and spend that period of ours very productively. In the other *hadith* concerning our topic, the Messenger of Allah decreed the following, "Allah the Almighty had taken away the opportunity of giving excuses for a person, to whom he gave a sixty-years-life."[38]

In fact, human beings are not perfect. That is why, Allah blessed us with life in order to compensate our shortages, and leave the Gates of Repentance open. In other words, He gave us an opportunity to repent from our lifelong mistakes. Despite that, if a person to whom Allah gave sixty years of life, spent his life not repenting from his sins and earning Allah's content, will not have even the slightest

---

[38]   *Sahih al-Bukhari*, Riqaq, 5

possibility of asking to be sent back in the Hereafter (to life to accomplish good deeds and earn Allah's good pleasure).

In fact, in addition to determining, this *hadith* points out the necessity of turning to Gates of Repentance before senility befalls and appraising our youth well so that we can be purified of our sins. It is definitely impossible to tuck the compensation of all of our mistakes, sins, and amiss acts in senility. In that case, we had better spend our youth and maturity in the rain of repentance and begging forgiveness, hence purifying ourselves.

At the same time, this *hadith* explains to us that if we do not repent and live our youth properly, then we should repent in senility for the wrong acts that we committed in our youth. However, no one knows where their life will end. This is why, we need to utilize this repository well and make use of the golden years of our lives. Perhaps, in youth, people commit most part of their mistakes and sins. The Messenger of Allah said, "After committing a sin, one should carry out a good deed immediately." The reason for this is to compensate for our mistakes and faults right away. This will be possible only by invigorating the youth (a period, when most of our faults are done). Particularly, failures made in a person's first years of self-consciousness may produce and give baneful results. There are plenty of sins, for which repentance is needed to be felt and uttered, whereas it could be so that a term of repentance had simply expired for that person. Well, we must not waste our youth (in such an extent that we will not have any excuses later), the most beautiful years of our lives, though there are many mistakes and committed sins, and instead of ignoring it with carelessness, we need to search ways for salvaging it.

Sixty years is more than enough time for arranging everything. However, it is necessary to denote that the given *hadith* does not mean that those, who had lived less than sixty years, have the right to give excuses in the Hereafter. Our Prophet stated that an average life term of the people of his community is sixty to seventy years. In a *hadith,* there was given the minimum limit of overall life term.

- 19 -

Advice of Our Prophet to His Young Companion

يَا عَبْدَ اللهِ، لاَ تَكُنْ مِثْلَ فُلاَنٍ، كَانَ يَقُومُ

اللَّيْلَ فَتَرَكَ قِيَامَ اللَّيْلِ

"O Abdullah! Do not be like so and so who used to pray at night and then stopped the Night Prayer." [39]

Worshiping Allah the Almighty requires perpetuation and perseverance on our behalf. There are some people, who have intentions of practicing religion with extreme ecstatic love at the time of their being surrounded in spiritual atmosphere or while their getting spiritual pleasure. In doing so, they set targets that they are incapable of carrying out. Throughout his whole entire life, the Messenger of Allah protected his community from having extremes. In other words, he protected his community from imbalances. The person, who narrated the given *hadith* and who was referred to as Abdullah was a Companion of the Messenger of Allah, Abdullah ibn Amr ibn As. He spent the entire year fasting. As soon as the Messenger of Allah found out about it, he asked him:

---

[39] *Sahih al-Bukhari*, Tahajjud, 19; *Sahih Muslim*, Siyam, 185

"Is it you who spent all year fasting?"

"Yes, o Messenger of Allah," he replied.

"No, you'd better not do that. You may fast only on Mondays and Thursdays."

"O, Messenger of Allah, I can manage fasting even more."

Seeing the perseverance of Abdullah, the Messenger of Allah said: "If so, then you may fast every other day but not every day of the year. This is the fasting of the Prophet Dawud, peace be upon him, the most acceptable in the eyes of Allah supererogatory fasting."

However, Abdullah ibn Amr concluded his words by saying, "I can do even more."

As the Messenger had already stated his last words and given his final decree, from then on, he started to fast, in the presence of the Messenger of Allah, all the time until the end of his life, excluding the religious festive days. However, the following words that were poured from his mouth show us how much he regretted having not listened to the advice of the Prophet: "If only I had listened to advice of the Messenger of Allah. That day I could accomplish a duty, which I have taken. But now it is very difficult for me. Moreover, I do not want to oppose a word given that I gave in the presence of our Prophet. That is why I have to do it now."

Young people usually have many goals that they are unable to fulfill. After all, an addressee of the *hadith* was a Companion named Abdullah ibn Amr ibn As. People should not set goals, the fulfillment of which are beyond their abilities. However, they should apply much effort to fulfill the planned. People, who achieved their ideals, are those, who aspired the loftiest goals of theirs. One needs to behave likewise in order to not get a stamp of "failing the agreement," at the end, i.e. not to act according to a given word.

Particularly, youth should continue carrying out their good deeds. Again, getting desperate and giving in fast happens mainly among young people who were not able to achieve their lofty goals.

Our Prophet in this *hadith* as well as in some other *hadith*s stated that the most praiseworthy of deeds are those ones, those that accomplish less but are continuous. One of the conclusions that we can make from this *hadith* is that a Muslim's, giving an idea of "possibility of leaving accomplishment of good deeds" is wrong from the point of view of conveying the message and enlightening people. If so, then all Muslims, and especially youth, should undertake only those goals that they are able to and should earn a habit of acts that he can always do easily.

Let's complete the explanation of this *hadith* with personal words of the son of Umar ibn al-Khattab and the brother-in-law of our Prophet, Abdullah describing the same matter, i.e. about the matter of continuing the already started religious practices:

Abdullah ibn Umar said: "Anytime when Companions of the noble Messenger of Allah had seen a dream, they used to come to him and tell it. I used to covet and wished to see a dream and then explain it to the Prophet. That time I was very young. I also used to sleep in the mosque (for, it became accustomed). Finally, my wish came true. In my dream two angels caught me and gulped me down to Hellfire. Hell was twined with stones like the inner side of wells. There were two other people (besides me). They were my familiars from the tribe of Quraysh. I got scared of the all seen and started to say: 'I take refuge in Allah from Hell.' At that moment, another angel approached me and said: 'Don't be scared!' I told my elder sister, Hafsa, about this dream, and she submitted it to the Messenger of Allah. Thereupon, the Messenger of Allah stated: 'What a good person Abdullah is! I wish he prayed the Tahajjud Prayer.' Since then, I spent my nights worshiping."[40]

---

[40] *Sahih al-Bukhari*, Tahajjud 2, 21, Fadailu's-Sahaba, 19; Ta'bir, 25, 36; *Sahih Muslim*, Fadailu's-Sahaba, 139, 140

-20-

A Youngster That Lived Hundred Years

خَيْرُ النَّاسِ مَنْ طَالَ عُمُرُهُ وَحَسُنَ عَمَلُهُ

"The best of people are those who live longest and excel in their deeds." [41]

𝒜 llah predestines everyone's terms of life. All our acts done in this world comprise our deeds. The best person is that, who is not only blessed with a long life, but also with a large amount of good deeds. As for being the best, a long life will not benefit you at all. In this *hadith,* it is said that a long life will earn value only with the presence of good deeds. From the *hadith,* it is indirectly understood that it's better to enhance good deeds during the prime of our lives instead of trying to do so in senility. Thereby, a person should pay great importance to the accomplishment of good deeds in his youth, so that, if he has a long life, to have an honor of being amongst the best people.

Being the "best" here is perceived from the perspective of relation of life and deeds. For, in other but alike *hadith* there is an additional statement of "The worst of people are those, who live long and have

---
[41] *Sunan at-Tirmidhi,* Zuhd, 21, 22

-21-

Youth and Cultural Degeneration

مَنْ تَشَبَّهَ بِقَوْمٍ فَهُوَ مِنْهُمْ

"Whoever resembles a people, he is one of them." [45]

his *hadith* enunciates to us that anyone who tries to look like representatives of other communities will be considered from them and judged accordingly. A Muslim should comply with customs and traditions of his own community, act according to his own cultural norms, and should present his attitude and manners in senses of his own civilization. Behavior of people under the influence of immorality today are seen in many areas of such matters as apparel, talking styles, family life, and relations with other people, is like a slavish mimicry.

The above mentioned matters are possible to consider within frames of the given *hadith*. Nowadays, by means of television, internet, and cinemas, our people, and especially our youth, have started to imitate some norms that belong to other cultures. Departing from an example of appearance, we may say that there are many

---

45 *Sunan Abu Dawud*, Libas, 5; Ibn Abi Shayba, *Musannaf*, 7:639; Abdu'r-Razzak, *Musannaf*, 11:454

among us, who want to imitate the outfits of actors that are seen in soap operas, who are interested in making the same hairstyles that are fashioned in movies, or even copy the attitude and manners of people (by different means). This very *hadith* shows us the wrongfulness of all those things. A Muslim is a person, who has his own values and tries to apply them. Here is perfect, contemporary example: in our society, it is not common or traditional to come in to a house with shoes. However, there are people, who become accustom and begin applying to their lives after seeing it in movies. If that situation is not considered to be emulation and imitation, then I don't know what is…

A point that we'd like to draw your attention to is the expression of *tashabbuh* (imitating, resemblance), mentioned in the *hadith*. Imitation will be possible only by severe dissimulation. There is no need to do so, because such insincerity will bring degeneration and abstraction of personal values, as well.

Truly, by departing from this *hadith* and looking at a subject, generally we may say that our religion takes care of apparel and distinct outfits of men and women. It is definitely worth mentioning here that colors of clothes have influence on human psychology and a fact of certain colors' being abominable should be appraised from that point of view.

-22-

Modesty and Youth

كَانَ رَسُولُ اللهِ صَلَّى اللهُ عَلَيْهِ وَسَلَّمَ أَشَدَّ حَيَاءَ مِنَ الْعَذْرَاءِ
فِي خِدْرِهَا، فَإِذَا رَأَى شَيْئاً يَكْرَهُهُ عَرَفْنَاهُ فِي وَجْهِهِ

"The Messenger of Allah, peace and blessings be upon him, was more shy than a virgin in her separate room. If he saw a thing which he disliked, we would recognize that (feeling) in his face." [46]

*I*n this *hadith*, not only the modesty of the Messenger is praised, but it is also understood that it is a characteristic that befits young people the most. It is a subtle coincidence that the narrator of the *hadith*, Abu Said al-Khudri, was one of the young Companions of the Messenger of Allah.

Truly, the noble Messenger would never say anything whenever he used to see something unpleasant, and he would never jump into someone's face and point fingers whenever that person did something wrong in his presence. Sometimes, people used to realize their mistakes by looking at the face of the Prophet. It was a novelty and characteristic that belonged to him, brought on behalf of the educational system that addressed the spirit and intellect at the same time.

---

[46] *Sahih al-Bukhari*, Manaqib, 23; Adab 72, 77; *Sahih Muslim*, Fadail, 67

At the age of puberty, a young girl, who had grown up in an Islamic environment, compared to before, starts to pay more attention to her outfit, speech, behavior in society, and spruce herself up. In doing so, her character becomes much more delicate and relations with other people become much more elegant. In the given *hadith*, the Messenger of Allah was compared with a girl similar to this description. That was done so because of his perfect manners and profound modesty. There are plenty of good examples of the noble Prophet concerning modesty and chastity of today's youth. At the time, when modesty and shyness were torn away and chastity was stepped all over, only by the help of the heroes of modesty and chastity, who resolved upon accomplishing Lord's commands sincerely, we regained the previous peace and tranquility that prevailed in our society in the past. Even modesty of a single youngster may result in high culmination.

Pious scholars give us the following explanation of modesty: "Modesty is a character of a person that keeps him from doing all kinds of evil deeds. It will provide fulfillment of all the duties that person has to others."

Junayd al-Baghdadi described it by saying: "Modesty is a state of seeing innumerable favors of our Lord and grasping shortcomings of ours before those favors."

Truly, shyness mostly resides in women due to their pure, noble, and emotional nature.

This nice feeling that exalts people's degrees was one of the most distinctive features of our beloved Prophet.

-23-

A Youngster That Spent His Youth Obeying to Allah

إِنَّ اللهَ يُحِبُّ الشَّابَّ الَّذِي يُفْنِي شَبَابَهُ فِي طَاعَةِ اللهِ

"Verily Allah loves the young man who spends his entire youth in the obedience of Allah."[47]

s a person gets older, two things related to him will get younger: One of them is his love and the other is his limitless wishes and desires... In that very *hadith* mentioned above, the Messenger of Allah denoted and mentioned to us a feature that Allah the Almighty loves in a young person: It is spending one's life, in the most active phases of life, when blood dementedly runs in one's veins and when one's carnal and sensual desires are at their peak, within the limit of worship and devotion to Allah. Instead of their dealing with lusts of their peers, they get advanced more and more in worshiping Allah. Without being proud with worldly wealth and by being away from guiles of their carnal selves and Satan, they make their times productive by performing religious practices. Truly,

---

[47] Abdullah ibn Mubarak, *Kitabu'z-Zuhd wa'r-Raqaiq*, 464; Ajluni, *Kashfu'l-Khafa*, 1:286, 748; Sahawi, *Maqasid al-Hasana*, 1:68; Ali al-Muttaqi, *Kanzu'l-Ummal*, 15:776

worship is desired and a wonderful thing for everyone, however, value of worship performed in youth is completely different.

Worships and righteous deeds bring an impermanent youth to a state of everlasting by spending it in bustling about Allah's content, carrying pumps and delivering buckets of water to people, whose faiths are ruined, and offering treats, which lead to Allah, to hungry hearts that live away from belief. Those are all the most important of religious practices that are to be done in a person's youth. For guiding a person in helping to find the right path is much virtuous than anything else in the Universe. This very thing was declared by the most trustful person, our Prophet.

As for those people who run after their wishes and desires in heedlessness and consider death to be a distant concept—by departing from this *hadith*, concept and dissidents, we may say that— Allah the Almighty does not love people like that. Young people, who wait for the last few moments of their lives to orienting themselves to the Hereafter, as if they have guarantees for living long, those who do not enliven faiths that rest in their hearts, head over heels in love to worldly things, are (possibly) among those youngsters, whom Allah does not love. However, Allah's Compassion and Mercy are infinite; He will not deprive those young people, who spent their past in similar manners but later found the Straight Path, by His Mercy, (surely) provided that they will repent and not have the lust that they used to have before.

The Messenger of Allah, in another *hadith,* stated, "Allah loves repenting youngsters." Repenting requires not committing the same sins again.

-24-

Relatives and Privacy

إِيَّاكُمْ وَالدُّخُولَ عَلَى النِّسَاءِ، فَقَالَ رَجُلٌ مِنَ الأَنْصَارِ
أَفَرَأَيْتَ الْحَمْوَ؟ قَالَ: الْحَمْوُ اَلْمَوْتُ

*"The Messenger of Allah, peace and blessings be upon him,
said, "Beware of getting, into the houses and meeting women
(in seclusion)." A person from the Ansar said: "O Allah's
Messenger, what about husband's brother", whereupon he
said: "Husband's brother is like death."* [48]

ere is another *hadith* concerning our topic of, "None of
you must stay alone with a woman, if one of her close
relatives is not there." [49]

A word of "halwat," mentioned in *hadith,* means "staying alone in
a company of a woman, whose close relative (with whom marriage
is religiously forbidden) is not there." From here, it is understood
that *halwat* is religiously forbidden.

If to have an abstract view of given *hadiths* it becomes clear that
one must abstain from being in the company of a woman, whose
husband, mother, father, son, brother, sister, aunt, or milk sibling are

---

[48] *Sahih al-Bukhari,* Nikah, 111; *Sahih Muslim,* Salam, 20
[49] *Sahih al-Bukhari,* Nikah, 111, Jihad, 140; *Sahih Muslim,* Hajj, 424

not present. If a man's sister, daughter, paternal, or maternal aunt is there, then it is considered that the woman's close relatives are present and their staying in one room under appropriate conditions will be allowed.

The beloved Prophet in this *hadith* emphasized the very importance of this matter, disregarded by many, in a conspicuous manner. By doing so, the Prophet merely informed us of a problematic situation that made up basis for awry relations. Herewith, relatives get comfortable. Those, who have alike situations, are more likely to commit that very mistake because they have an opportunity to drop in and leave off at any time. A word, mentioned in (the Arabic text of) the *hadith*, "alhawmu," which means, "the male relatives of husband," comprises of such individuals such persons as brother of husband, his nephew, uncle, and children of the uncle. These relatives must be more cautious than strangers are. For, usually, they do not get together with strangers anyway. As for male relatives of the husband, then they do feel free in visiting; hence, they are subject to becoming victims of Satan.

In various narrations of this *hadith,* the very reasons for that danger are given quite obviously by the statement of the Prophet: "The third one of them is Satan." It will not be opposed to amplifications and deceptions of Satan based on male or female trial. Therefore, we should always remember that Satan is given as an example of blood that runs in veins of people, especially, youth.

Here, we need to mention and remark that a condition of *halwat* will not be considered so unless doors are locked and curtains are veiled in places that are usually open to everyone. However, caution and measure should always accompany a believer, due to the fact that ill-intentioned people are everywhere. Particularly, if we were to consider the very complicated life conditions of today, the importance of being away from *halwat* comes out to be very distinctive and very crucial.

In another *hadith,* our noble Prophet decreed, "The wives of those, who went to strive in Allah's cause and for humanities good, are like mothers to those, who left behind." In doing so, he stated that family members of those, who migrated to foreign lands to convey the message and exalt the Name of Allah, are like mothers to those, who were left behind. After saying this, the Messenger of Allah turned to his Companions and, to underline and emphasize the importance of that matter, he said: "Definitely, it is so. What else did you think?"

Truly, in this *hadith* it is said about a very significant measure taken for purifying society from immorality by blocking all ways that lead to committing adultery.

-25-

Emulation and Trying to Look like Individuals of Opposite Sex

لَعَنَ رَسُولُ اللهِ صَلَّى اللهُ عَلَيْهِ وَسَلَّمَ الْمُتَشَبِّهِينَ مِنَ الرِّجَالِ بِالنِّسَاءِ، وَالْمُتَشَبِّهَاتِ مِنَ النِّسَاءِ بِالرِّجَالِ.

"The Messenger of Allah, peace and blessings be upon him, cursed the women who imitate men, and the men who imitate women." [50]

$\mathcal{B}$y mentioning other *hadith*s concerning our topic, we will try to explain this one: According to Abu Hurayra, the Messenger of Allah condemned women, who dress up like men, and men, who dress up like women.[51]

According to another *hadith* narrated by Abu Hurayra, the Messenger of Allah stated, "There are two categories among the inhabitants of Hell whom I have not encountered. The first are people who carry whips like the tails of cows and beat the people with them. The second are women, clothed yet naked, drawn to licentiousness and enticing others to it, their heads like the swaying humps

---

[50] *Sahih al-Bukhari,* Libas, 61, 62; *Sunan Abu Dawud,* Libas, 28; *Sunan at-Tirmidhi,* Adab, 24; *Sunan ibn Majah,* Nikah, 22

[51] *Sunan Abu Dawud,* Libas, 28; Ahmad ibn Hanbal, *Musnad,* 2/325

of camels—they will neither enter Paradise nor even smell its fragrance, though its fragrance can be found to a great distance."[52]

A matter that is forbidden in *hadith*s is, in fact, emulation to the opposite gender. It may be manifested either by attitude, apparel, or speaking style. However some people are free concerning their apparel, speech, and attitude; they are prone to emulate and resemble persons of the opposite sex. Such a happening denotes to us the matter explained in the *hadith*.

It is worth mentioning here that apparel does not consist of a simple outfit, as it is most often perceived. A huge portion of retrogression starts from seemingly insignificant apparel. Even nowadays formation of unisex outfit style that fit men and women instigate emulation. The only way of getting rid of it is to take serious warnings of our noble Prophet.

As for the women who look unclothed while being clothed, many people would agree that they are ungrateful people, who do not thank the Lord for granting them favors, those, who comparatively do comply with covering parts of their bodies but dress immodestly to enchant their beauties, those, whose body features become clear because of their thin and transparent clothing, those, who outwardly follow norms of covering but in their souls and hearts are "uncovered," who infringe limits of honor and chastity put by Allah because they do not pay heed to them and, moreover, they try to attract other women to their circle, those, who try to attract men's attention with their coquettish manners and stunning attitudes and those unfortunate women, who are enthusiastic about resembling men, look mannish, primordial natures of whose suffer deformation.

Here we witness such features of the noble Prophet as giving the most concise remarks, ability of saying meaningful things in brief, as well as his statement concerning two groups of women that will come in the future but were not at his time.

---

[52] *Sahih Muslim*, Jannah, 52

-26-

Tongue and Private Parts

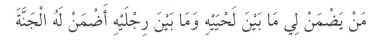

مَنْ يَضْمَنْ لِي مَا بَيْنَ لَحْيَيْهِ وَمَا بَيْنَ رِجْلَيْهِ أَضْمَنْ لَهُ الْجَنَّةَ

"Whoever can guarantee (the chastity of) what is between his two jaw-bones and what is between his two legs (i.e. his tongue and his private parts), I guarantee Paradise for him." [53]

This noble *hadith* tells to us all to protect our tongues along with our private parts. The Messenger of Allah will serve as a guarantor of entering into Paradise for those, who promise to protect those parts of their body.

Tongue is an invaluable and precious part of our body, but if it is used in the wrong way, it may turn into a dangerous device that will lead a person to tribulation, and will finally devastate a person. Using their tongues, people can glorify Allah, ordain goodness, abstain from evil, recite the book of Universe and the Holy Qur'an, its eternal interpreter, and convey the message to others. Sometimes, because of a tongue, a disbeliever may start believing. Because of a tongue, a person may attain the highest position in Paradise. The same tongue may drag a person to scourge. A tongue may be means of cursing as well as gossiping and slander. Namely this is

---

[53] *Sahih al-Bukhari*, Riqaq, 23; *Sunan at-Tirmidhi*, Zuhd, 60; Ahmad ibn Hanbal, *Musnad*, 4:398, Hakim, *Mustadrak*, 4:397–399

why the Messenger of Allah said: "Do use your tongues in lawful domain in order for me to promise you Paradise."

By not mentioning the name of the genital organ, the Messenger of Allah said, "what is between his two legs," and in doing so, he manifested his sublime manner and etiquette. After all, the Messenger of Allah always had profound morality. While talking about private parts that might make others uncomfortable (shameful), he, out of his beautiful conduct and respect, used to allude to them as, "what is between his two legs."

The space between a person's two legs is a great trial for all of humanity. As continuation of generation goes through that way, adultery, licentiousness, and dilapidation of generation, too, goes through the same way. The evil usage of private parts will mix up genealogies of all. Chastity is directly connected to conserving families and surviving nations. While chaste people and generations born from these people continue their spiritual structures till the Day of Resurrection, individuals and nations that sunk in the swamp of adultery and licentiousness will not carry their existence even to coming generations.

The Messenger of Allah promised Paradise to those, who gave a word concerning their tongues and private parts. Attainment here is in difficulty of protecting those parts of the body. For, at times when corporal desires cover entire body, fathom ourselves and afflict our souls and even when our willpower weakens and gets opened to all kinds of evil, it is very important to restrain ourselves for the sake of Allah. It will be means of increase of spiritual levels. The person, who was able to do that deed, will definitely be guaranteed by the Messenger of Allah and fly onto Paradise.

Truly, a person, who can repress gushes of his carnal self at moments when all kinds of evil deeds and temptations surround him, put it under the discipline, refuse to with patience and continuously concentrates his forces on such frailties, will be able to attain a spiritual benediction in a single moment while others would deserve it during long years. Such an act will let him earn even more rewards at a time than a person, who prayed a thousand-unit Prayer. Furthermore, it will let him go towards (the point of) sainthood in an upright position.

The Messenger of Allah told with a concise expression about ways that lead to Paradise and in doing so, he gave us an etalon of ideal individual and community.

-27-

Hell Is Surrounded
by Temptations

حُفَّتِ الْجَنَّةُ بِالْمَكَارِهِ وَحُفَّتِ النَّارُ بِالشَّهَوَاتِ

*"Paradise is surrounded by hardships, and the Fire is
surrounded by desires."* [54]

*I*t is said that Paradise is surrounded with unpleasant things
because people are prone to look and weigh everything in
materialistic matters; hence, their eyes may consider them
to be bad. Many things that lie on the way to Paradise are not from
a category that attracts people who look for evil. It happens like
this because of apparent views of our minds (in this world). By accomplishing things that our carnal selves find difficult, people can
(literally) fly to Paradise. An expression of "The most beautiful of
deeds are those that carnal selves find difficult" emphasizes the
above said in the best way.

Contrary to Paradise, Hell is surrounded with things that our carnal selves find pleasing. A feature of having no limit to wishes and
whims that lead to Hell demonstrate themselves. Keeping in mind
this *hadith*, it is quite possible to say that a person, who does what-

---

54 *Sahih al-Bukhari*, Riqaq, 28; *Sahih Muslim*, Jannah, 1

ever relates to his corporal and carnal desires, is surely following a path that leads directly to Hell.

Truly, the atmosphere around Hell seems to be very charming. Almost everything that pleases people, doing whatever our carnal selves wish to, surround Hell and even serve as the perimeter.

As for Paradise, it is surrounded with taking ablution, performing Daily Prescribed Prayers and the Hajj, giving purifying alms, enduring and tolerating difficulties, being deprived of human rights, and other similar things. All these things are considered to be unpleasant things from when looked at from modern perspectives. If to look at things that surround Paradise and Hell through a veil, then (we will see that) Hell is surrounded with seductive things and Paradise with heavy ones. Therefore, many people look at the outer view of things and are deceived. Hence, there are very many candidates of Hell; however, those who demand Paradise are considerably less.

"Hell is like a witch that made a trap from simple ambitions. Truly, lust is a poisonous honey. We may resemble people to moths, flying in a veering position to flames, where they would perish. Like them people do go mindlessly towards lusts that surround Hell and later would find themselves in a blazing fire. As they cannot exactly tell what is there behind the veil; everything that veiled Hell would birch their corporeality and drag them towards itself. That a fact the Messenger of Allah explained with his next *hadith*: 'The metaphor of me and people is like a man who lights a fire and when it lights up what is around it, the moths and other creatures begin to fall into it. He begins to drive them away from it, but they overpower him and rush into it. I take hold of the knots of your waist-wrappers to keep you back from the Fire while you are rushing into it.'[55]

Let us state that most of people are in pursuit of inconsiderable accounts. A person, who says: "Prayer is good but performing it five times a day is difficult for me," gets stick to a tiny difficul-

---

[55] *Sahih al-Bukhari*, Riqaq, 26; *Sahih Muslim*, Fadail, 17–19

ty of Prayers. Many were stranded by difficulty of taking ablutions in winters. However, the same ablution would take gradually a person, who performed it despite its small difficulty, to Paradise. The same is for fasting, paying purifying alms and performing the Hajj. Many of people, whose intellects do not let them to act intelligently, do not fulfill necessary bounds because of tiny obstacles and unevenness. Hence, all unpleasing things around Paradise become obstacles for them."[56]

---

[56] Gülen, M. Fethullah, *Muhammad: The Messenger of God*, New Jersey: Tughra Books, 2012

-28-

Youth and Pilgrimage

عَنْ لَقِيطِ بِنِ عَامِرٍ رَضِيَ اللهُ عَنْهُ، أَنَّهُ أَتَى النَّبِيَّ صَلَّى اللهُ

عَلَيْهِ وَسَلَّمَ، فَقَالَ: إِنَّ أَبِي شَيْخٌ كَبِيرٌ لاَ يَسْتَطِيعُ الْحَجَّ، وَلاَ

الْعُمْرَةَ، وَلاَ الظَّعَنَ، قال: «حُجَّ عَنْ أَبِيكَ وَاعْتَمِرْ»

*Laqit ibn Amir came to the Messenger of Allah, peace and blessings
be upon him, and said: "My father is a very old man and does not
have strength to perform Hajj or Umrah or to undertake the journey."
He replied: "Perform Hajj and 'Umrah on behalf of your father."* [57]

Relating to this very topic, we will mention two more *hadith*: Said ibn Yazid, may Allah be pleased with him, narrated: "At the age of seven, at the time of the Farewell Pilgrimage, I also made pilgrimage to Mecca together with the Messenger of Allah." [58]

Here is another *hadith*: According to the narration of Ibn Abbas, may Allah be pleased with him, the Messenger of Allah met a group of people at the place called Rahwa.

---

[57] *Sunan Abu Dawud,* Manasik, 25; *Sunan at-Tirmidhi,* Hajj, 87; *Sunan an-Nasa'i,* Manasik, 2, 10; *Sunan ibn Majah,* Manasik, 10

[58] *Sahih al-Bukhari,* Sayd, 25

"Who are you?" asked he.

"We are Muslims but who are you?" inquired they.

"I am the Messenger of Allah," replied the noble Prophet.

A woman held up a child of hers to the Prophet during Hajj and said, "O Messenger of Allah, is there Hajj for this one?"

He said, "Yes, and you will be rewarded."[59]

Let's convey one more *hadith* concerning our topic: At the Farewell Pilgrimage, when the Messenger of Allah travelled from Muzdalifah to Mina in company of the elder son of Abbas, Fadl, who was behind Prophet's mount, a young woman from the tribe of Khath'am approached the Prophet. On one hand there started conversation (in the form of question and answer) between the Messenger of Allah and the woman and on the other hand the young women and Fadl ibn Abbas started to have a glance at one another. When the Messenger of Allah noticed that, he turned the head of Fadl to other side. The woman said, "Allah's command, concerning the obligation of Pilgrimage, is a given right at the time, but my father got too old; he cannot sit up on a mount because of senility." She revealed weakness of her dad and told that she wanted to perform the Hajj on his behalf. The Messenger of Allah decreed: "Yes, you may." His positive reply is a proof for delegation for Hajj.

In this noble *hadith*, many things are decreed concerning permissions of making pilgrimage for the weak and incapable people, via vicegerents, preventing exchanging of glances with one another (concerning men and women) by Prophet's turning Fadl's face away and necessity to obstruct, any religiously forbidden thing, for elders. However, here we'd like to emphasize on children's ability to go on pilgrimage instead of their parents, recommendation of visiting those sacred places in childhood and youth, the duty of children and youth of taking care of their parents, serving them,

---

[59] *Sahih Muslim*, Hajj, 409, 410, 411

paying their debts and if necessary, making pilgrimage to Mecca instead of them.

Truly, young people experience completely different feeling at sacred places like Mecca and Medina. Familiarization of children to such religious practices as Daily Prayers and other acts of worship is necessary and of vast importance. In the same way, their getting used to Pilgrimage and making Pilgrimage together with your children is to the point and virtuous.

One more thing that we can fathom from these specific *hadiths* is that the pilgrimage of small children is permitted and authentic. Alongside with this, those, who can afford going on Pilgrimage as adults, their Pilgrimage made in childhood will not be enough. They must fulfill their obligatory Pilgrimage. This does not mean that parents are not rewarded for taking their children on the Hajj. There is a vast, Divine reward for the parents and the children that go on Pilgrimage.

-29-

Youth and Learning
World Languages

عَنْ زَيْدِ بْنِ ثَابِتٍ قَالَ: أَمَرَنِي رَسُولُ اللهِ صَلَّى اللهُ عَلَيْهِ
وَسَلَّمَ أَنْ أَتَعَلَّمَ لَهُ كَلِمَاتٍ مِنْ كِتَابِ يَهُودَ. قَالَ إِنِّي وَاللهِ
مَا آمَنُ يَهُودَ عَلَى كِتَابِي. قَالَ فَمَا مَرَّ بِي نِصْفُ شَهْرٍ حَتَّى
تَعَلَّمْتُهُ لَهُ قَالَ فَلَمَّا تَعَلَّمْتُهُ كَانَ إِذَا كَتَبَ إِلَى يَهُودَ كَتَبْتُ
إِلَيْهِمْ وَإِذَا كَتَبُوا إِلَيْهِ قَرَأْتُ لَهُ كِتَابَهُمْ

*Zayd ibn Thabit narrated: "The Messenger of Allah, peace and
blessings be upon him, ordered me to learn some statements
from writings of the Jews for him, and he said: 'For indeed by
Allah! I do no trust the Jews with my letters.'" He said: "Half
a month did not pass before I learned it, when he wanted to
write to the Jews I would write it to them, and when they wrote
to him I would read their letters to him."'* [60]

---

[60] *Sahih al-Bukhari*, Ahkam, 40; *Sunan Abu Dawud*, Ilm, 2; *Sunan at-Tirmidhi*, Is-
tizan, 22; Ahmad ibn Hanbal, *Musnad*, 5:182; Hakim, *Mustadrak*, 3:477;
Tabarani, *Al-Mujam al-Kabir*, 5:155–156

The Messenger of Allah, who informed us that our religion will be spread all over the world, virtually drew attentions on the fact that will provide fulfillment of that ideal. Nowadays, the message that we convey to humanity depends on dialogue, and the most irrevocable element of it is language. In fact, by giving Zayd ibn Thabit the command to learn Hebrew, the Messenger of Allah was also giving us the same message. We must remember that the best period, when one can pick up the language and put it into practice, is during their youth.

Knowledge of language will assure proper information interchange in a communication circle. The Messenger of Allah, who taught many methods of teaching and schooling, in this *hadith* recommended to us to learn world languages. Today, learning the world languages is a significant responsibility for the sake of serving humanity.

-30-

Spiritual Life

إِنَّ الْحَلاَلَ بَيِّنٌ، وَإِنَّ الْحَرَامَ بَيِّنٌ، وَبَيْنَهُمَا مُشْتَبِهَاتٌ لاَ يَعْلَمُهُنَّ
كَثِيرٌ مِنَ النَّاسِ، فَمَنِ اتَّقَى الشُّبُهَاتِ، اسْتَبْرَأَ لِدِينِهِ وَعِرْضِهِ،
وَمَنْ وَقَعَ فِي الشُّبُهَاتِ، وَقَعَ فِي الْحَرَامِ، كَالرَّاعِي يَرْعَى حَوْلَ
الْحِمَى يُوشِكُ أَنْ يَرْتَعَ فِيهِ، أَلاَ وَإِنَّ لِكُلِّ مَلِكٍ حِمًى، أَلاَ وَإِنَّ
حِمَى اللهِ مَحَارِمُهُ، أَلاَ وَإِنَّ فِي الْجَسَدِ مُضْغَةً إِذَا صَلَحَتْ صَلَحَ
الْجَسَدُ كُلُّهُ، وَإِذَا فَسَدَتْ فَسَدَ الْجَسَدُ كُلُّهُ: أَلاَ وَهِيَ الْقَلْبُ

*"Both legal and illegal things are evident but in between them there are
doubtful (suspicious) things and most of the people have no knowledge
about them. So whoever saves himself from these suspicious things
saves his religion and his honor. Whoever indulges in these suspicious
things is like a shepherd who grazes (his animals) near the Hima (private
pasture) of someone else and at any moment he is liable to get in it. (O
people!) Beware! Every king has a Hima and the Hima of Allah on the
earth is His illegal (forbidden) things. Beware! There is a piece of flesh in
the body if it becomes good (reformed) the whole body becomes good
but if it gets spoilt the whole body gets spoilt and that is the heart."* [61]

---

[61] *Sahih al-Bukhari*, Iman, 39; Buyu, 2; *Sahih Muslim*, Musaqat, 107, 108

ue to its extensive meaning, this *hadith* is considered to be one of five *hadiths* that comprise the essence of Islam. This *hadith*, which encloses permitted, forbidden, and doubtful actions and gives instructions on handling them, advices to and commands Muslims to keep away from doubtful things. It warns that some Muslims may consider that at young ages people may act in a "freewheeling" manner concerning doubtful things, unknown by many and are hard to distinguish at first glance between permitted and forbidden.

In fact, this happens because of lack of knowledge. By comparing these matters to other subjects, i.e. giving critical interpretations, pious Muslim scholars do clarify them. There is a general principle, agreed on by many of the most well-known scholars: "Leave what makes you doubtful for what does not." Therefore, it is dangerous to circulate around doubtful things." The *hadith* warns us to keep away from everything doubtful. Not being meticulous in those matters makes us find ourselves in a "grey zone" of forbidden actions. It would make us wretched. We would be talked about by people and be objects of scorn. Above all, we would lose Allah's consent. If we avoid doing doubtful things, we would protect our faith and chastity, reputation and honor.

By accepting doubtful subjects, which have no certain decrees on regarding their being permitted or forbidden, and matters, which are considered to be abominable by pious scholars, as permitted and practicing them without hesitations, we may unwittingly be lead to forbidden areas.

When explaining doubtful matters, the Messenger of Allah reminded his Companions of the matters of some Arab Rulers. They would never permit anyone to enter their private groves and gardens, where they pasture their own herds. They used to give severe punishments to those, who disregarded that rule. After which the Messenger of Allah decreed that Allah, too, had His own restricted areas, i.e. forbidden grounds. Those, who enter into those areas, would be considered as ones, who defied Him.

At the end of the *hadith*, the heart is referenced. Spiritual welfare of heart depends on its being nourished with religiously permitted things and its finding peace by remembering Allah, the All-Compassionate. Those who pay no attention to permitted and forbidden rules and wander about restricted areas would definitely have no regular spiritual health and (sound) relationship with Allah. This is a serious complication, which would cause deterioration of the entire body and soul.

-31-

Good Manners

أَدَّبَنِي رَبِّي فَأَحْسَنَ تَأْدِيبِي

"Allah gave me good manners (adab), and He rendered my manners in the best way." [62]

"dab" is an Arabic word for literature, which has a wider frame of connotation associated with good manners, gentleness, elegance, refinement, and perfection. It has often been interpreted in relation to a person's lifestyle, conduct, and integrity and as a means to the flourishing of that person in spirituality and purification of the heart. The Messenger of Allah is the paragon of *adab*. No matter which meaning of the word *adab* is considered as far as this hadith is concerned, good manners or power of expression, the Messenger of Allah is always the epitome of both.

One day Abu Bakr asked the Prophet: "O Messenger of Allah! Who gave you such good manners?" The Prophet replied: "Allah gave me good manners and He rendered my manners in the best way."

Aisha, the daughter of Abu Bakr and the wife of the Prophet, was asked about the morals of the Prophet. She replied: "Don't you ever read the Qur'an?" Her audience answered to the affirmative. She then continued: "His morals were the Qur'an."

---

[62] Ali al-Muttaqi, *Kanzu'l-Ummal*, 7:214

The Prophet was granted such great manners by the Creator that he reached the peak of morality; those who seek the real meaning of manners should examine the courteous Prophet's actions and behavior and transfer this into their own way of living.

Allah created His Messenger with the greatest manners and behavior, as a model to all mankind; on the contrary, it is difficult to imagine the great burden that the noble Prophet shouldered with such a mission. He carried the responsibility of all his followers. If Prophet Muhammad, peace and blessings be upon him, had not been endowed with such exalted mannerism it is likely that he would have made errors in his behavior like any ordinary person; however, unlike the rest of us, his mistakes would have been reflected and amplified by his followers. The noble Prophet was not answerable for himself alone; rather, he shouldered the responsibility for his entire community. This is why Allah created His Messenger with outstanding morals and behavior and sent Him as a beautiful example for mankind.

Prophet Muhammad, peace and blessings be upon him, was known for his good deeds and actions; sometime prior to his Prophethood, restoration work was being carried out in Ka'ba. The Messenger helped the workers to repair and rebuild the holy house. His uncle Abbas threw his gown over his shoulder to prevent any stones from injuring him. He saw that the Prophet's shoulder was grazed and sore from the heavy stones, so his uncle advised him to do the same; however doing so would have exposed the upper part of his thigh (which was later forbidden by Islam). Suddenly an angel appeared before him and the Prophet fainted, falling to the ground. He never again contemplated on such a thought, for he was under the protection of the Creator, even well before his Prophethood.

The Prophet once said: "I had the intention of taking part in a wedding ceremony when I was young, and on both occasions I was overpowered by sleep; when I woke up the wedding had long finished."

These are all events that happened before he was blessed with the Prophethood. Throughout his lifetime Allah never gave his Messenger any reason or the opportunity to commit any inappropriate action in any way; this is an exceptional condition that was granted to the Prophet alone.

It is not surprising that this was the case, for when he was a young child his chest was opened by the angels and any tendency or trace of evil was removed. The target of the Devil's arrow, the black spot that is found in every human heart, was removed from the Prophet's heart when he was very young. The Devil instigates within us apprehension and suspicion, he runs through our veins, impelling us to evil; but he was unable to even approach Allah's Messenger, for he was an exceptional person.

The Almighty never gave his Messenger the chance to do evil or to sin, either prior to or during his Prophethood; he lived a life of purity from the day he was born until he departed from the universe and he was the embodiment of good manners.

The good manners and behavior of Prophet Muhammad, peace and blessings be upon him, remained with him throughout his entire life; his every move or action reflected his virtuous manners. Although it was a rare occasion, the Prophet became upset or frustrated upon certain cases, but this too was due to his good manners as well. There was always a valid reason for his anger, and it was in response to injustice.

A Bedouin came to the Prophet while he was with the Companions and harshly pulling at the Prophet's collar, demanded justice; the Bedouin pulled the Prophet's collar so hard that a mark remained on his neck. This greatly upset the Companions, but the Prophet just smiled and told him in a calm voice, "Give this man what he asks for." This event is one of the hundreds of examples that indicates the depth and breadth of the beloved Prophet's great tolerance.

There are many situations in which even the most sedate person justly becomes annoyed or frustrated, but even under these conditions the morals of the Prophet shone through like the gleaming sun. The following is just one of the most dramatic examples:

The Prophet had dream shortly before setting out for the Battle of Uhud; this dream led the Prophet to believe that remaining in Medina and forming a defensive battle would be more appropriate, and he approached the Companions saying, "We should remain in Medina." However, the Companions were so excited and keen to fight for the sake of Islam that such excitement clouded their judgment.

So they set off for Uhud, with the Prophet personally taking command and organizing the army in the best possible way; the enemy began to flee after the first attack, but the archers had not grasped the fine point of obeying the Prophet's command accurately and abandoned their posts.

As a result, sixty-nine Muslims was martyred, among them the Prophet's uncle Hamza; every man on the battlefield was injured and some of them carried the pain of these wounds for the rest of their lives. But even more importantly, the greatest injury for the Muslims was that the honor of Islam had been damaged.

Such behavior by an army would have angered any other leader and under normal circumstances the Prophet could have treated those around him harshly; but Allah the Omniscient prevented the Prophet from acting harshly, protecting and guiding him. Allah revealed:

> It was by a mercy from Allah that (at the time of the setback), you (O Messenger) were lenient with them (your Companions). Had you been harsh and hard-hearted, they would surely have scattered away from about you. Then pardon them, pray for their forgiveness, and take counsel with them in the affairs (of public concern); and when you are resolved (on a course of action), put your trust in Allah. Surely Allah loves those who put their trust (in Him). (Al Imran 3:159)

The Prophet was a person who commanded great respect; indeed, the Merciful One addressed His Messenger in the same way. For instance, instead of saying "Do not be harsh hearted," the Creator addressed the Prophet, revealing: "Had you been harsh and hard-hearted," that is, "you are not harsh."[63]

---

[63]   *40 Hadiths*, Ali Budak and Korkut Altay, New Jersey: Tughra Books, 2011, pp. 38–41

- 32 -
Piety, Kindness and Good Behavior

اتَّقِ اللَّهَ حَيْثُمَا كُنْتَ وَأَتْبِعْ السَّيِّئَةَ الْحَسَنَةَ

تَمْحُهَا وَخَالِقِ النَّاسَ بِخُلُقٍ حَسَنٍ

*"Fear Allah wherever you are. Follow up a bad deed with
a good deed and it will blot out the former, and deal with
people in good manners."* [64]

There is nothing like good manners to exalt one. Good behavior is a virtue of Allah and a good-mannered person is one who has been blessed with the virtues of the Creator. The above hadith explains the path to piety and the concept of protecting piety in our everyday lives; it is such a vast subject that it would take many books to rightfully illustrate its true significance.

"Taqwa" is the Arabic word for piety, and means duly fearing Allah, while pious people are called "muttaqi;" the guide for these people of wisdom is to live within the boundaries and regulations set by Allah and Prophet Muhammad, peace and blessings be upon him, to live in moderation, avoiding both excess and deficiency. *Taqwa*, like any other action in the life of a believer, must be a guide

---

[64] *Sunan at-Tirmidhi*, Birr, 55; Ahmad ibn Hanbal, *Musnad*, 5:153

in the right direction; as in everything else, a Muslim should keep a balanced line at *taqwa*. Setting up difficult principles beyond the frame of the tradition of the Messenger of Allah and pushing others to practice these principles means going beyond the boundaries of religion.

To elaborate on this point, one should avoid forcibly imposing supererogatory Prayers in addition to the Prescribed Prayers; rather, they should stress the significance and merits of optional worship and encourage others about it. For example, we may consider that the Night Prayer is necessary, because it is the path to seeking Allah's pleasure, the way to Paradise, and an enlightenment of the soul. This is why in the darkness of the night we stand before the Creator of all when we are alone. At the same time, one should not forget the importance of continuously remembering the Creator and glorifying the One Who has granted us so many blessings in the world. In fact, this constant flow of benevolence and grace that Allah has bestowed upon us deserves gratitude and thankfulness in our words, actions and behavior; if we were to refrain from showing gratitude and instead ignored the blessings that the Creator has sent us then we might be subjected to Divine punishment. This is stated in the following verse from the Qur'an: "*If you are thankful (for My favors), I will most certainly give you more; but if you are ungrateful, surely My punishment is severe*" (Ibrahim, 14:7).

This is the reason why the continuance of supererogatory worship, whether it is Prayer or expression of gratitude, should be considered to be part of our daily duty. In addition, the words of those who worship devotedly will make it far more understandable and acceptable for others.

Another important aspect of taqwa that needs great care and attention is that which is permissible and that which is forbidden according to Islam; those who ignore the restrictions or live without taking care will never reach the truth of piety. When they read the Qur'an they will not be able to realize its importance or the invigoration its verses invokes in the human soul. This Divine book is the path to piety; a book which has guided pious ones to faith. The principle characteristic of a pious person is that they avoid that which is forbidden and fulfill the obligatory aspects of faith.

It is possible to say that a person's perception of the world plays a great role in reaching true piety; the world motivates human beings in two directions, towards good or towards evil. The Prophet said: "The world is like a prison for a believer and Paradise for the unbelievers." Human beings come in this world once and they see the fruits of their worldly life displayed before them in the Hereafter. This is why acknowledging the real value of the blessings in this world, our youth, health, wealth, and life and utilizing these blessings in the best possible way is necessary; these blessings are the means of gaining everything we require in both this world and the Hereafter.

Of course, there are many unfortunate people who, despite having everything, are blind to the true value of the blessings that have been bestowed upon them; they are like fish living in the ocean, unaware of the true value of the sea until they are swept onto the beach. A human being must live in this world and, regardless of all else, must have a constant awareness of the eternal life of the Hereafter.

Another significant point in acquiring taqwa or reaching a new dimension in the scope of taqwa is retreating from the routine duties of daily life and occupying ourselves with activities that spiritually intensify human contemplation. We should also feed our minds with relevant reading and return to our duties with refreshed vigor and work efficiently. Organizing such spiritual gatherings and spending time for them are vital dynamics for our life in both worlds, irreplaceable by anything else.

The following verse from Qur'an expresses another characteristic of those who reach true piety, telling us that they are those who:

...remember and mention Allah (with their tongues and hearts), standing and sitting and lying down on their sides (whether during the Prayer or not), and reflect on the creation of the heavens and the earth. (Having grasped the purpose of their creation and the meaning they contain, they conclude and say): "Our Lord, You have not created this (the universe) without meaning and purpose. All-Glorified are You (in that You are absolutely above doing anything meaningless and purposeless), so save us from (having wrong conceptions of Your acts and acting against Your purpose for creation, and so deserving) the punishment of the Fire! Our Lord! Whomever You admit into the Fire, in deed You have brought him to disgrace. (Having concealed or rejected Allah's signs in the heavens and on the earth, and so denied Allah or fallen into associating partners with Him), the wrongdoers will have no helpers (against the Fire). Our Lord! Indeed We have heard a caller calling to faith, saying: 'Believe in your Lord!', so we did believe. Our Lord, forgive us, then, our sins, and blot out from us our evil deeds, and take us to You in death in the company of the truly godly and virtuous. Our Lord! Grant us what You have promised us through Your Messengers. Do not disgrace us on the Day of Resurrection; indeed You never break Your promise. (Al Imran 3:191–194)[65]

---

[65] *40 Hadiths*, Ali Budak and Korkut Altay, New Jersey: Tughra Books, 2011, p. 54

- 33 -

The Surprises Awaiting
the Righteous Servant

قَالَ اللّٰهُ أَعْدَدْتُ لِعِبَادِي الصَّالِحِينَ مَا لَا عَيْنٌ رَأَتْ وَلَا أُذُنٌ سَمِعَتْ
وَلَا خَطَرَ عَلَى قَلْبِ بَشَرٍ

*"Allah the most exalted said: I have prepared for My righteous
servants what no eye has seen and what no ear has heard,
nor has it occurred to the human heart"* [66]

This *hadith* refers to a surprise for believers, speaking of the most unexpected things arriving at the most unexpected times. Although Qur'an mentions some of the blessings that await the faithful ones, humans will be unable to understand the reality and true value of the existence of these until they attain them.

In his interpretation of a verse (al-Baqarah 2:25) of the Qur'an, concerning the fruits of Paradise, Ibn Abbas states that these things are fruits that human beings have not experienced before but that when we taste them we will be reminded of something that we have eaten in the past. These are not the same fruit that we have here, for the fruit of Paradise has been created in conformity with the eternity

---

[66] *Sahih al-Bukhari*, Tawhid, 35; *Sahih Muslim*, Jannah, 4

and immortality of Paradise itself. Thus, seeking the fruit of this world in Paradise would be nothing less than simplemindedness.

Paradise is a place of surprises; another one of the surprises of Paradise is reunion with the Creator, for the thousands of years of life in Paradise. This bliss beyond imagination awaits the sincere believers of servitude.

The *salih* (righteous) ones mentioned in the hadith are those who fully perform actions free from flaws while *salihat* (good deeds) are the actual actions that are performed to perfection. The only way to understand if actions are flawless is to compare them with the Divine criteria; that is, how is the Prayer performed according to the Divine commands, how do we fast and give in charity, how do we struggle in the way of Allah, how do we control our ego, how do we elevate the soul, how do we strengthen our willpower and how do we develop our emotions and feelings? All these questions are subjected and assessed according to Divine regulations; therefore, in the first stage towards perfection, a human being must calculate and regulate their actions according to the Divine declarations so that they will give pleasure and delight to their Creator. Like the musician who takes great care in tuning his instrument to please the audience we must prepare ourselves prior to standing before the Creator according to the commands of the Qur'an so that we will be among those who are favored by Allah.

Another explanation of *salihat* (good deeds) is that, these actions should be done to the best of our ability, with the awareness of seeking Divine approval. As believers we must make every effort to fulfill the duties that have been bestowed upon us, since which exact actions of ours will be the means to our salvation cannot be defined or known. This is the reason Prophet Muhammad, peace and blessings be upon him, said: "Fear Allah and never disparage (underestimate) a good deed."[67]

---

[67] *Sunan Abu Dawud*, Libas, 25

In addition, the Merciful One speaks of: "My righteous servants" in the hadith. Righteousness brings people closer to Allah and they become His beloved servants. Allah's affection for His servants is expressed in another hadith: "When I love (a servant) I am his ears with which he hears, his eyes which he sees, his hand with which he strikes and his foot with which he walks."[68]

Therefore, a servant who continuously performs good deeds comes so close to their Creator that their every action is under Divine guidance; can you imagine, a devoted believer is guided towards the path of truth with every step they take? Such a person can only be one who turns to their Creator, towards Divine beneficence. Such a person has reached the status of "My righteous servant," and is accepted as one who has reached Divine affiliation. Such a person constantly pleas with their Lord: "O Allah! Hold me and guide me for I am nothing without You!"

Giving water to a thirsty dog can sometimes be the means of entering Paradise, while depriving a cat of food can lead to Hellfire.[69] Attaining Paradise and the rewards given in Paradise is a total surprise, a Divine mystery. We can only recognize the things we actually see or hear in this world. Actually, our imagination is also limited by the capacity of our senses here. Therefore, it is not possible for us to fathom the blessings in an infinite realm.

Another aspect could be that the Creator rewards our good deeds sometimes ten, a hundred, or seven hundred times over or more but it is impossible for a believer to know the reward that awaits them. Thus, when we are awarded for our deeds in the Hereafter we will be amazed, as the merits bestowed upon us are beyond our imagination.[70]

---

[68] *Sahih al-Bukhari*, Riqaq, 38

[69] *Sahih al-Bukhari*, Anbiya, 54

[70] *40 Hadiths*, Ali Budak and Korkut Altay, New Jersey: Tughra Books, 2011, p. 105

Sources

Abdullah ibn Mubarak, *Kitabu'z-Zuhd wa'r-Raqaiq*, Daru'l-Kutubi'l-Ilmiyya, Beirut, nd.

Abdu'r-Razzak ibn Hammam, Abu Bakr as-San'ani, *Al-Musannaf*, Al-Maktabu'l-Islami, Beirut, 1403.

Al-Ajluni, Abu'l-Fida Ismail ibn Muhammad, *Kashfu'l-Khafa wa Muzilu'l-Ilbas amma ishtahara mina'l-Ahadisi ala Alsinati'n-Nas*, Daru'l-Kutubi'l-Ilmiyya, Beirut, 1988.

Ahmad ibn Hanbal, Abu Abdillah Ash-Shaybani, *Musnad*, Muassasatu Qurtuba, Cairo, nd.

Ali Al-Muttaqi al-Hindi, *Kanzu'l-Ummal*, Muassasatu'r-Risala, Beirut, 1989.

Al-Ayni, Abu Muhammad Mahmud ibn Ahmad, *Umdatu'l-Qari fi sharhi Sahih al-Bukhari*, Daru Ihyai't-Turasi'l-Arabi, Beirut, nd.

Al-Bayhaqi, Abu Bakr Ahmad ibn Husayn ibn Ali ibn Musa, *As-Sunanu'l-Kubra*, Maktabatu Dari'l-Baz, Mecca, 1994.

..................., *Shuabu'l-Iman*, Daru'l-Kutubi'l-Ilmiyya, Beirut, 1410 H.

Bazzar, Abu Bakr Ahmed ibn Amr ibn Abdulhaliq Al-Basri Bazzar, *Musnad* (Al-Bahru'z-Zahhar), Maktabatu'l-Ulum wa'l-Hikam, Medina, 1995.

Al-Bukhari, Abu Abdillah Muhammad ibn Ismail al-Ju'fi, *Al-Jamiu's-Sahih*, İstanbul, 1401 H.

Canan, İbrahim, *Kütüb-i Sitte Tercüme ve Şerhi*, Akçağ Yayınları, İstanbul.

Abu Dawud, Sulayman ibn Ash'as as-Sijistani al-Azdi, *Sunan*, Daru'l-Fikr, Beirut, nd.

Abu Nuaym, Ahmad ibn Abdillah al-Isfahani, *Hilyatu'l-Awliya wa Tabaqatu'l-Asfiya*, Daru'l-Kitabi'l-Arabi, Beirut, 1405 H.

Abu Ya'la, Ahmad ibn Ali al-Mawsili, *Musnad*, Daru'l-Ma'mun li at-Turas, Damascus, 1984.

Al-Hakim an-Naysaburi, Abu Abdillah Muhammad ibn Abdillah, *Al-Mustadrak Ala's-Sahihayn*, Daru'l-Kutubi'l-Ilmiyya, Beirut, 1990.

Erul, Bünyamin, "Hz. Peygamber ve Gençlik," sonpeygamber.info

Gülen, M. Fethullah, *Fasıldan Fasıla*, Nil Yayınları, İzmir, 1996.

..................., herkul.org, "Kırık Testi"

.................., *İnancın Gölgesinde-2*, Nil Yayınları, İzmir, 1992.

.................., *Kırık Testi-7: Ölümsüzlük İksiri*, İstanbul, 2009.

.................., *Sonsuz Nur-1*, Nil Yayınları, İzmir, 1993.

.................., *Zaman*, "Kürsü sayfası," 21.12.2007.

Heyet, *Riyazu's-Salihin*: Peygamberimizden Hayat Ölçüleri, Erkam Yayınları, İstanbul, 2001.

Heyet, *Riyazu's-Salihin (Muhtasar)*, Işık Yayınları, İstanbul, 2009.

Haythami, *Majmau'z-Zawaid wa Manbau'l-Fawaid*, Daru'l-Fikr, Beirut, 1412 H.

Haythami, Nuraddin and Harith ibn Abi Usama, *Musnad al-Harith*, Markaz al-Khidmati Sunna, Medina, 1992.

Ibn Abi Shayba, Abu Bakr Abdullah ibn Muhammad al-Kufi, *Al-Musannaf fi'l-Ahadis wa'l-Athar*, Maktabatu'r-Rushd, Riyad, 1409 H.

Ibn Majah, *Sunan*, Daru'l-Fikr, Beirut, nd.

Karagöz, İsmail, *Aile ve Gençlik*, TDV Yayınları, Ankara, 2005.

"Al-Maktabatu'sh-Shamila" 2.11, http://www.waqfeya.net/shamela

Al-Munawi, Zaynuddin Muhammad Abdu'r-Rauf, *Fayzu'l-Qadir Sharhu'l-Jamii's-Saghir*, Daru'l-Kutubi'l-Ilmiyya, Beirut, 1994.

Muslim, Abu'l-Husayn ibn Hajjaj al-Qushayri an-Naysaburi, *Sahih Muslim*, Muqaddima, Daru Ihyai't-Turasi'l-Arabi, Beirut, nd.

An-Nasa'i, Abu Abdirrahman Ahmad ibn Ali ibn Shuayb, *As-Sunanu'l-Kubra*, Daru'l-Kutubi'l-Ilmiyya, Beirut, 1991.

.................., *Sunan*, Maktabatu'l-Matbuati'l-Islamiyya, 1968.

Al-Qudai, Abu Abdillah Muhammad ibn Salama ibn Ja'far Qudai, *Musnad ash-Shihab*, Muassasatu'r-Risala, Beirut, 1986.

Said ibn Mansur, Abu Osman ibn Shuba al-Hurasani, *Sunani Said ibn Mansur*, Daru's-Sami'i, Riyad, 1993.

As-Sahawi, Abu'l-Khayr Shamsuddin Muhammad ibn Abdirrahman, *Al-Maqasidu'l-Hasana fi Bayani Kathirin mina'l-Ahadisi'l-Mushtahira Ala'l-Alsina*, Daru'l-Kitabi'l-Arabi, Beirut, 1994.

As-Suyuti, Abu'l-Fazl Jalaladdin Abdu'r-Rahman ibn Abi Bakr, *Al-Jamiu's-Saghir fi Ahadisi'l-Bashiri'n-Nazir*, Daru'l-Kutubi'l-Ilmiyya, Beirut, 1990.

At-Tabarani, Abu'l-Qasim Sulayman ibn Ahmad, *Al-Mu'jamu'l-Kabir*, Maktabatu'l-Ulum wa'l-Hikam, Musul, 1983.

At-Tirmidhi, Abu Isa Muhammad ibn Isa, *Al-Jamiu'l-Kabir (Sunan)*, Daru'l-Gharbi'l-Islami, Beirut, 1996.

Wensinck, A.J., et. al., *Al-Mu'jamu'l-Mufahras li Alfazi'l-Hadisi'n-Nabawi*, Çağrı Yayınları, İstanbul, 1988.

Zaghlul, Abu Hajar Muhammad Said ibn Basyuni, *Mawsuatu Atrafi'l-Hadisi'n-Nabawiyyi'sh-Sharif*, Daru'l-Fikr, Beirut, 1994.